# REASONS

# REASONS

## Recapturing the WHY of Reaching the Unreached

**Jack Nelson**

Worldlink International Ministries
Valley Forge, PA

**Reasons:**
Recapturing the WHY of Reaching the Unreached

**Jack Nelson**
Worldlink International Ministries
Valley Forge, PA

© 2023 by Worldlink International Ministries
All rights reserved

Worldlink International Ministries
PO Box 80202, Valley Forge, PA, 19484, USA
www.worldlinkonline.org

Cover design by Josh McGuire
Back Cover quote by Michael Hyatt:
©2018, Full Focus.
All rights reserved.
Originally published at fullfocus.co

ISBN 978-0-9982646-1-5

First printing 2023

Printed in India

# DEDICATION

To the Church of Jesus Christ; His Bride; His Body; His Beloved: You welcomed me in when Jesus welcomed me in. You nurtured my young faith when it needed to be formed. You informed my head and heart through countless encounters with the Scriptures and those who know and teach them well. You inspired me with visions of who our wondrous God is and what He did, is doing and could do. You broke my heart more than a few times and yet you are beautiful because you are becoming more and more like the Savior in whom we both live. This book is an ever-so-small offering expressing my unquenchable gratitude and my ardent longing for your continual joy and transformation.

# CONTENTS

# PREFACE
## Recapturing the WHY

King Solomon opined that *"there's nothing new under the sun."* *(Ecclesiastes 1:9)* I'm not sure that this volume will prove him wrong. He also said, *"Of making many books there is no end, and much study wearies the body." (Ecclesiastes 12:12)* (Thanks, Sol, you are such an encouragement to authors).

All right, my hermeneutic purity requires me to admit that neither of those verses has a direct interpretation applying to this book. However, they are somewhat applicable.

It does seem, especially in this digital and social media world, that everyone and their brother, sister, and distant relative have a new forum to create "content" on every subject imaginable. And maybe they have done so.

So why write another book? Why write *Reasons*?

After I wrote *Reachable: How Indigenous Missionaries Are Changing the Face of Missions*, I saw the eager acceptance of indigenous missionary partnerships within a group of Christians who already had an understanding of the privilege and responsibility of sharing the love of God and Good News of Jesus with those who had never had the opportunity to hear, understand and respond to it.

But I realized in church after church, conference after conference, conversation after conversation that a good number of Christians, even committed and passionate ones, were not seeking the answer to HOW to reach the world for Jesus because they had never asked the question WHY reach the world for Jesus.

This struck me as I would be in conversations in church lobbies after I preached and watched people walk by a table offering a free copy of *Reachable*. (Now, I must confess that I'm not sure I ever rejected the offer of a free book… except those offered by certain cults which I encountered at my front door or in airports during my early ministry days). I love to learn new things when I don't have the answer.

I asked myself, and sometimes asked others, "Do all these really wonderful people believe that they already know the answer to how to reach the unreached for Christ… or are they not even asking the question?"

Author Michael Hyatt, speaking in a business context said, "People lose their WAY when they lose their WHY."

I fear that, in the mission that God gave us to reach the world for him, some of us have lost our WHY!

So, I think that it is important that we remind ourselves of some core truths if we have heard them before and expose ourselves to those same truths if we have never heard them before.

What I share here may not be new, or revelatory. Virtually everything I say in this book has been said by somebody else (and probably said better). It is, for many of you readers, a restatement of that which you have heard for years. In fact, you may have heard it so many times that it has lost its power to shock your senses or jolt you toward action.

For many years I played guitar. I picked it up as a teenager to help lead worship at a Christian youth camp and I played it through years of children's ministry, youth ministry, and even church planting ministry. For years, I practiced and played many times a week to prepare and serve. As time went on, there were others who were more talented than I (it was not hard to find them) and they would take over the playing and my Yamaha FG 350W would go back into the basement until a need arose and no one better was available.

For nearly 20 years, that meant that I would ignore the guitar from August until May. As summer approached, I knew that I would spend weeks leading teams of young people on summer outreach ministry to children and youth. I would pull out the faithful guitar and put some new strings on it. Then, with little preparation, I would jump in front of the crowd and bang out my astonishing repertoire of 3-chord kid's songs that were laid aside after the previous summer.

Year after year I would rediscover the strange thing that happened to the fingertips of my left hand. From August to May they became soft. As I started playing each new summer, the strings that dug into my fingertips hurt. A lot! I wanted to change; to do something different.

Over the first few weeks of each summer, as I played through the pain, I developed calluses where the strings touched the fingers. As the weeks went by, the calluses got thicker and thicker until I felt no discomfort and hardly any pressure.

By repeated exposure, I became able to basically ignore the presence of the sharp metal guitar strings which earlier had caused both acute discomfort and a seemingly irresistible urge to change my behavior.

This book (more accurately, the truth that I pray that God will express to you through it) might be like guitar strings. Your reaction will have everything to do with whether you have developed calluses.

For many who will read *Reasons*, this is "old stuff." You've heard it before. You've been to church. You've attended mission conferences. You've read books or articles on reaching unreached people. You could probably teach these things better than I can. You are in particular danger.

If you've been playing this instrument for many years, you may have calluses on your heart that could prevent the sting of these truth-strings from causing sufficient enough discomfort to motivate a change of mind and heart and to initiate action.

My encouragement to you, and prayer for you, is that before you read *Reasons* you will sit with your Lord and ask him to create in you a soft heart. That you would plead with God to pierce you anew with the truth of his word. Ask him to reveal if what you will read is true, and if so, what he wants you to do with this knowledge.

But I'm convinced that there are many in a second group of people who will read this book. For you, you've either never heard these things or, if you have heard them, you've never HEARD them.

Maybe you recently came to faith in Christ. Maybe you recently started seriously thinking or studying about how to live as a Christ-follower. Maybe you came out of a religious system where you thought, or were taught, that ministry to unreached people was someone else's job; the professionals, wealthy donors, the "church", Western missionaries, or some particular church leader.

Today might be the first time in your life that you hear someone with biblical authority say, "No, it is not solely someone else's responsibility. It is your job, also. God commissioned you to play a unique and vital role; to have an essential part in his unfolding drama of redemption."

God's invitation to make an eternal difference in the lives of those who have yet to hear about his Good News is still valid. This book contains some of the reasons why I believe those of us who claim to be serious followers of Jesus must accept his invitation.

I pray that, in this book's pages, you will rediscover the "WHY" of reaching the unreached.

# ACKNOWLEDGEMENTS

*God is not unjust; he will not forget your work and the love you have shown him as you have helped his people and continue to help them. (Hebrews 6:10)*

Thousands of men and women have helped make this book a reality. They have taught these truths by word and by witness. They have given me the privilege of being their friend and co-laborer. They are Worldlink's courageous indigenous missionary partners on the front line of ministry. They are our dedicated Home Team who serve tirelessly to make that ministry possible. They are Worldlink's sagacious Board of Directors who set the clear course for our ministry ship. They are generous stewards of God's resources who share to provide the fuel that propels our missionaries forward to reaching the unreached. They are faithful prayer warriors whose intercession may never be noticed but will always be felt.

Thank you. Without you, this book does not exist.

I particularly want to thank Chuck, who has been my steadfast ministry partner for the last decade and a half when God has poured out his blessing on Worldlink's work; Maddie, who has labored to get this book from my thoughts to your hands; and Mark, who has been a "spiritual buddy" for many years and has made both me and this book better.

# INTRODUCTION
## Get Ready, Get Set...

We're going to play a word-association game: I'm going to give you a word and I want you to think of the first words that come to your mind when I say that word. Ready? (That wasn't the word.)

The word is…. Jesus. Go for it.

What were the first words that came to your mind?

God. Son. Savior. Redeemer. Servant. Lover. Powerful. Alive. Friend. Healer. Judge. Revealer. Giver. Example. Almighty. Compassionate. Deliverer. Divine. Forgiver. Holy. Glorified. Immaculate. Incorruptible. Just. Almighty. Omnipotent. Omniscient. Perfect. Trustworthy. Truth. Way. Life. Vine. Gate. Door.

No doubt, there are innumerable words that you could have brought up if given sufficient time. When you hear of Jesus you have a mind that is full of understanding about who He is.

You may attend a Christian church where, year after year, they have been building brick-by-brick, story-by-story, fact-by-fact, Biblical passage-by-passage, a remarkably complete concept of who Jesus is. So, immediately recalling words about Him is almost second nature.

Let me try another word. Same game. I give you a word and you think of the first few words that come to your mind when I say that word.

The word is… Katteholeyamma. Go for it.

Done already? This one is a little harder because you likely have never heard of Katteholeyamma. You have no ability to bring to your mind or your mouth an image or a word to associate. Does it have something to do with a woman named Kate? Katteholeyamma has the word hole in it; did she fall in a hole? Yamma sounds like llama. Is it a pit dug by an Andean woman named Katherine to catch stray camelid pack animals? Actually, no.

Why do I bring up Katteholeyamma (who, you can be forgiven for not knowing, is a minor goddess among the 330 million Hindu deities)? I want to make a point that is splendid in its simplicity: You cannot bring to mind someone of whom you have never heard. (And now the word "duh" may come immediately to your mind, but sorry no prize because we have concluded our word-association game).

Let me say it again. **You cannot bring to mind someone of whom you have never heard**.

Let me put it another way that relates to the theme of this book: You cannot respond in faith to a person of whom you have never heard.

Jesus said, *"I am the way, the truth and the life. No one comes to the Father except through me." (John 14:6).* To come into a relationship with God the Father, or as the Bible calls it to be "saved," a person must come to Jesus. To come to Jesus, a person must know about Jesus.

Paul the apostle put it this way in his letter to Christians in Rome: *"Everyone who calls on the name of the Lord will be saved. How, then, can they call on the one they have not believed in? And how can they believe in the one of whom they have not heard?" (Romans 10:13-14).*

Here is where the games cease, and the reality becomes literally deadly serious.

There are over 8 billion people in our world composed of 17,438 distinct people groups according to Joshua Project. Almost 3.4 billion people in 7,382 of those groups would be categorized as unreached and living with limited access to the good news about Jesus. Nearly 2 billion of our world's inhabitants live where there are no known gospel movements and less than 0.1% Christians.

This means there are well over a billion people in our world who would lose badly at our word association game with "Jesus" because they have never heard of Jesus. And billions more who live essentially isolated from any realistic way to learn about who Jesus is, what he did for them, and what he offers them.

Those are the "Unreached" people I talk about when I say, in this book's subtitle, "Recapturing the WHY of Reaching the Unreached."

So, you ask, "Why?" I'm glad you asked.

In the next chapters, I want to go through some very familiar and some less familiar Biblical texts and tell you why I think that I, and you if you are a Christ-follower, must be involved in some way with bringing the Good News of Jesus to people who have never heard it.

Now, let me take a quick parenthesis and address very directly two groups of people who might be reading this book.

First, I know that in any group of readers, there are very possibly some people who would say, "You know what? I don't really know about this Jesus. I've never really heard clearly who he is and what he's done, and I've never gotten to the place where I really understood all this to the point where I can call myself a Christ-follower like you just mentioned."

If you are in that group, I'm going to just admit off the bat that this book is really not written for you. It is written for people who have faith in Christ; to people who have heard and examined the bold historical claims of Jesus, looked at the line of faith, and said "I'm stepping over. I'm in. I'm going to trust and follow him."

But, while admitting that this book is designed to address Christians, here's what I'm going to say to you if you are not one: I am so deeply glad that you are reading *Reasons*. I am thrilled! My deepest hope and my sincerest prayer is, that by reading on you will see something new about the loving heart of God for you and others who have yet to step over that line of faith. My heartfelt desire is that you'll see something about the deeply flawed yet loving heart of Christians for you and others in your situation. And that you'll grow with a new understanding and appreciation for both God and Christians.

Perhaps you'll sense a deep inward whisper of God inviting you to respond to his love and his offer to come to him. After that, you may just join those of us who are working to assure that everyone has a chance to understand who Jesus is and to respond to his call to trust and follow him. So, again, I am so, so deeply glad that you are reading. If, at any point, you want to understand more about what Jesus is offering, just stick a bookmark where you are reading and flip back to Appendix 1 at the end of the book. Hopefully, that will make it clear.

But there is another group of potential readers. You may be a Christ-follower but have, for any number of reasons, a struggle with grace. You probably don't struggle with grace for salvation, and you probably don't struggle with grace for others. But, if you are like many good people I know, you have a struggle with grace for yourself. If that is you, then you are in particular danger in reading *Reasons*.

That danger is because you may encounter in the following pages many ways in which you fall short of the way that God commands you to live and then you may be tempted to look at yourself with condemnation. Do not fall into that pit!

I cannot and will not take the time to explain the grace of God to you, but I will proclaim it over you from Romans 8:

*Therefore, there is now no condemnation for those who are in Christ Jesus, because through Christ Jesus the law of the Spirit who gives life has set you free from the law of sin and death...*

*What, then, shall we say in response to these things? If God is for us, who can be against us? He who did not spare his own Son, but gave him up for us all - how will he not also, along with him, graciously give us all things? Who will bring any charge against those whom God has chosen? It is God who justifies. Who then is the one who condemns? No one. Christ Jesus who died more than that, who was raised to life - is at the right hand of God and is also interceding for us. Who shall separate us from the love of Christ? Shall trouble or hardship or persecution or famine or nakedness or danger or sword? As it is written:*

*"For your sake we face death all day long;*
*we are considered as sheep to be slaughtered."*

*No, in all these things we are more than conquerors through him who loved us. For I am convinced that neither death nor life, neither angels nor demons, neither the present nor the future, nor any powers, neither height nor depth, nor anything else in all creation, will be able to separate us from the love of God that is in Christ Jesus our Lord.*

Understanding, and responding to the things you will see in this book will not change the love God has for you. Nothing you do or fail to do will change that. If you are a believer in Christ, then you are God's child and dearly beloved. So, do not ever succumb to the internal (and infernal) pressure to try to live up to the convictions that God brings you in order to try to earn God's grace, salvation, or favor. We do not respond to the moving of God's conviction in order to be loved or saved, we do so because we are already loved and saved.

A great skill for a Christian is the ability to hold two truths at the same time. Yes, I have failed and also, yes, God, because I am in Christ, does not see me as a failure but as forgiven and righteous.

Listen, I live my life every day to advance the ideas you will read in the rest of this book, yet I find myself repeatedly falling short. My choice, and yours, is to either live in regret, shame, and paralysis or live in truth, grace, and action.

I am not sure if it is apocryphal or not, but John Newton, the reformed slave trader and author of Amazing Grace, is quoted as saying, "I am not what I ought to be, I am not what I want to be, I am not what I hope to be in another world; but still I am not what I once used to be, and by the grace of God I am what I am."

My prayer for you is that, as you read *Reasons*, you will hear God's voice and after reading and responding to his gracious loving prompts, you will say, "I am not what I used to be."

Now, back to the original question: WHY should I get involved in reaching the unreached? Let me give you ten REASONS.

# Part One

## REASONS

# Chapter - 1
## THE COMMAND OF CHRIST

Jesus' last commands on earth are recorded for us and with slightly different emphasis five times in the history books of the Bible's New Testament. (Matthew 28:18-20, Mark 16:15-16, Luke 24:44-49, John 17:18, 20:21, Acts 1:8).

These recorded events occurred in space and time. They are not just a story, they are history. And as has been said, "History is HIS story."

After Jesus, as fully God, had come to earth and taken on the clothing of full humanity being born to a young, poor, virgin in first-century Israel. After he lived a sinless and remarkable life during 30 years of obscurity as he *"grew in wisdom and stature, and in favor with God and man" (Luke 2:52).* After he launched a never-before-or-since rivaled public ministry of teaching with authority. After he demonstrated his authority over nature, over illness, over demonic forces, and over death. After he willingly died, having taken upon himself the sins of the world, and vicariously (in our place) paying the price required to offer each of us both forgiveness now and a place in heaven forever. After he was resurrected from the dead, proving his identity to the world, and confirming his new life offer to his followers. After he was prepared to ascend back to heaven and his eternally rightful place of honor. After all of that, Jesus had one last chance to give his followers instructions before he left them.

3

You'd think he, being omniscient God, would choose the most important topic for his parting words, his final sentences, his last command. And if you thought that, you'd probably be right! Matthew records:

*Then Jesus came to them and said, "**All authority** in heaven and on earth has been given to me. Therefore, go and **make disciples of all nations**, baptizing them in the name of the Father and of the Son and of the Holy Spirit, and teaching them to obey everything I have commanded you. And surely **I am with you always**, to the very end of the age." (Matthew 28:18-20)*

These words have come to be known as "The Great Commission." But what's so great about the Great Commission? Let's dissect Matthew's account of Jesus' commission and glance at the other historical writers' narratives and see four aspects of its greatness.

## GREAT IN ITS AUTHORITY

*Then Jesus came to them and said, "**All authority** in heaven and on earth has been given to me."*

How much authority? All!

All authority in which places? In heaven and on earth! In other words, in all places.

Given to whom? Jesus says, "Me!"

Whoa, cowboy, slow down a bit. That's a pretty brash statement.

In the North American culture where I live, we don't respond well to some one simply declaring their authority over us. We fought wars over that. We sing songs with lyrics like, "I did it my way." We quote poems with lines like, "It matters not how straight the gate, how charged with punishments the scroll. I am the master of my fate: I am the captain of my soul."

You may be reading this book from a different cultural lens or on a different continent's lands far from mine, but if you spend some honest time examining your desires and decisions, I think you will find at least a hint of that same self-lifting spirit. I think the Bible calls it "sin." It is the rejection of the law, the rule, the authority of God, and the substitution of my own reign in my life. So, let's all admit we have that tendency.

We want to be the ones with authority. We want to be able to make our own choices and go in our own direction.

But Jesus starts the Great Commission with a clear and unashamed reminder of his authority. Authority is the starting place for any commission. Without authority, this would be the Great Suggestion. The Great Option. The Great Menu Item that you can take or leave or substitute as you choose.

So, why does Jesus get to have all authority?

Let's look at Colossians 1:15-20 for some insight.

*He is the exact image of the invisible God, the firstborn over all creation. For by him all things were created: things in heaven and on earth, visible and invisible, whether thrones or powers or rulers or authorities; all things were created by him and for him. He is before all things, and in him all things hold together. And he is the head of the body, the church; he is the beginning and the firstborn from among the dead, so that in everything he might have the supremacy. For God was pleased to have all his fullness dwell in him, and through him to reconcile to himself all things, whether things on earth or things in heaven, by making peace through his blood, shed on the cross.*

5

Jesus gets all authority because he is the **Creator God** (v 15-16).

Let's dissect this a little bit. Jesus is the exact image of the invisible God. The word denotes a mirror-like representation. When you see Jesus, you see God even though God is invisible. And he is pre-eminent over all creation. As *Helps Word Studies* says, he is the "unequivocal sovereign over all creation." Why does he get to be sovereign over all creation? Because *"all things were created by him and for him."*

I was created by Jesus and for Jesus. You were created by Jesus and for Jesus. The world was created by Jesus and for Jesus.

The world was created by him and for his pleasure. God was not created by us and for our pleasure. Because He created us, he has the authority to tell us what to do.

Jesus gets all authority because he is the **Sustainer** (v 17).

Not only did Jesus start it all. He keeps it all going. He pre-existed creation and once he created, he became the cosmic glue that keeps molecules from flying apart.

Jesus gets all authority because he is the **Head** of the church (v 18).

The head of any body directs the body. The head is the leader, the ruler, the king, the boss. I heard an old preacher address Jesus this way, "You the boss, I the hoss. You crack the whip, I make the trip." That is a proper relationship of a body to the head.

Jesus gets all authority because he is the **Savior** (v 19-20).

We who were separated from God because of our sinfulness and our choice to be the Captain of our Soul were reconciled (changed in order to bring us together) to God. How? Jesus made peace through his blood shed on the cross. He paid the price!

Implicit in the Bible's explanation of salvation is the concept of redemption. Because he paid the price for our peace, that price purchased us. That's why Paul can write in I Corinthians 6:19-20, *"You are not your own, you were bought with a price."*

We are purchased. And the purchaser of anything has authority over the thing purchased. If I go out and get in my car to go to a meeting, I do not expect the car to decide to drive me to the beach (even though the beach might be really nice). And I don't expect someone else to tell me I can't drive my car to the meeting. It's my car. I bought it. I own it. I have authority over it. I can tell it what to do and where to go.

Because Jesus paid the price for me, he is the **Owner.** I am owned, and he is owed. He has the authority to tell me what to do and I owe him my submission.

Submitting to Jesus' authority was a decision I made on June 2, 1975. It was my graduation night from high school. I sat on the edge of my bed with my crimson cap and gown draped over my lap and without an audible voice, but with an impression that was clear as any physical voice I'd heard, Jesus invited me to, *"Choose this day whom you will serve." (Joshua 24:15)*

For nearly 50 years I've worked at submitting to his authority and have done so with truly remarkable imperfection.

I believe that Jesus starts the Great Commission with his authority because unless I am ready to submit to the authority of Jesus Christ as God, Creator, Sustainer, Head, Savior, and Owner, then I will look at his mandate, consider the potential cost, and walk away.

7

So, the Great Commission starts with great authority. Then it continues with a great mission.

## GREAT IN ITS MISSION

Therefore, go and ***make disciples*** … baptizing them … and ***teaching them to obey everything*** *I have commanded you…*

The great mission of the Great Commission is to lead people to be disciples of Christ; followers of him with faith and maturity. Faith is demonstrated by being baptized. Maturity is demonstrated by obeying Jesus' teaching.

The stated intention of the Great Commission is that this generation of believers see to it that this generation of unbelievers is given the opportunity to be the next generation of saved and growing believers. Nothing will impact eternity more.

Could anything be a greater commission?

There are any number of things to which people in our culture, nation, and era are committing their lives. I would dare to say that these are things to which people are giving away their lives.

It does not take much of a detective to observe humans, even religious humans, who are giving their one and only life for greater possessions. For greater prominence. For greater pleasure. For greater popularity. None of those is inherently evil, dark, or malicious. In fact, having a bit of any of those can be inherently beneficial.

The problem comes when they become the goal of our lives or the source of meaning in our lives. The issue becomes an issue when someone so loses sight of God's call, God's commission, for their lives that they begin to believe that any of these things are more than tools to use to accomplish God's mission.

# GREAT IN ITS SCOPE

It is interesting that the different men who, inspired by the Holy Spirit, recorded accounts of the times that Jesus shared his Great Commission recorded different words for the great scope of the mission.

In Matthew 28 we read: *Therefore, go and make disciples of **all nations...***

The Greek word for all nations is all "ethne" or ethnic people groups.

In Mark, we read: *He said to them, "Go into **all the world** and preach the good news to all creation…" (Mark 16:15)*

The word used for all the world is "kosmos" often used for all the world's systems.

In Acts, we read: *He said to them: It is not for you to know the times or dates the Father has set by his own authority. But you will receive power when the Holy Spirit comes on you; and you will be my witnesses in Jerusalem, and in all Judea and Samaria, and to the **ends of the earth."** (Acts 1:7-8)*

The word used for ends of the earth is "ges" (pronounced ghay) and means all soils or lands or regions.

Though not a recounting of the Great Commission, Matthew 24 records Jesus' answer to a question about his return at the end of time. One sign of this time, he reveals, is that *"this gospel of the kingdom shall be preached to the **whole world** as a testimony to the nations, and then the end will come." (Matthew 24:14).* The word translated world there is "oikoumene" which means all inhabited places of the earth.

Take all four of those concepts and put them into a single sentence describing the scope of where Jesus is commanding that his followers make new disciples and it may read something like this: *I want you to bring the good news of my love and the offer I make of salvation and a growing relationship with me to every person in every people group living under every social system in every inhabited place on every piece of dirt in the world.*

So, who does that leave out? Yep, no one.

The great scope of the Great Commission is unlimited. Unlimited by geography. Unlimited by language. Unlimited by political restrictions. Unlimited by time constraints. Unlimited by personal inadequacy. This brings us to the last great thing about the Great Commission.

## GREAT IN ITS PROMISE

When most of us think of the immensity, the importance, the greatness of the Great Commission and compare it to our personal smallness and shortcomings, we tend to shrink into a corner and ignore the clear command. We are tempted to say, "The task is too big, and I am too small. God, you have underestimated the assignment and overestimated the assignee. I cannot do it!"

Well, here is some good news and a dose of reality: you're right, you can't!

Jesus never expected us to slog through the mission trenches alone and with only our own power, perseverance, and self-effort. We cannot just read the commission, resolve to complete it, and screw up the self-disciplined chutzpah to "git-er-done". We cannot plan and program and perform our way to the prize. Even though the commission is given to us, trying to fulfill the commission in

10

our feeble strength is an unmistakable recipe for failure. Isn't that encouraging? Keep reading.

Right after giving the great mission of great scope with great authority, Jesus gives a great promise: *"And surely **I am with you always** even to the very end of the age." (Matthew 28:20b)*

"I am with you!" The only way that a commission this great can be accomplished is with a promise this great; the promise made by Jesus that he will be with us every step of the way.

Jesus' promised presence gives us the assurance of ultimate success and the knowledge of ultimate victory.

Back in the 1970s, there was a popular bumper sticker that declared: "God says it. I believe it. That settles it." There was even a song with those lyrics that you can look up and marvel at on a YouTube video. Though it may seem quaint at best and trite at worst, it has a ring of truth when it comes to the Great Commission.

Why should I be active in doing my part to reach the unreached with God's Good News? God said it! That should settle it and be enough for me to reorient my life to follow his authoritative command. That should be all we have to say (but, that would make for a remarkably short book, wouldn't it).

Is that enough for you?

"If so, get to it." If not (or if you're interested in some further bolstering of your resolve) read on and let's look at our second reason to reach the unreached.

# Chapter - 2
# THE RIGHT THING TO DO

You now know the command of Christ and that should end the discussion, right? If you need more to chew on, how about the simple truth that sharing the saving Good News with those who do not know it is simply the right thing to do?

I want to take you to an obscure passage from the bible's Old Testament in the book of II Kings. I would encourage you to read the whole passage (II Kings 6:24-7:9) in your bible when you can.

Before looking at the text, let's look at the context. You may have heard it said that when you take a text out of context you are left with a con. Let's never do that.

For context, starting in II Kings 6:24, we find that Ben Hadad, the king of Syria (or Aram) has mobilized his army and was coming to lay siege to Samaria where the king of Israel ruled. In that day, about eight centuries before Christ, advancing armies had several distinct ways of overtaking a city. As the king of an attacking force, you could go for the full-frontal attack on the city. In this strategy, the offensive force would get to the city and simply assault the city from the best angle. This was a legitimate strategy, especially if time was of the essence.

If you, as the attacking king, feared that a prolonged battle would raise the chances of reinforcements arriving to support the city's inhabitants, or if there was the need to move on rapidly to the next city on the to-conquer-this-campaign list, then the frontal attack was the go-to plan.

But there were some expected costs for this model. Most sizable cities of this era had a well-developed and effective defense mechanism, namely a wall. The wall, which would likely be several stories high and thick enough to support much of the protective army on its top, was designed to restrict city access to those who were invited and protect the inhabitants from those who were not.

The frontal attack required the army to go over or through the wall. A king who sent his army to scale a well-fortified wall could anticipate a long list of casualties as the defending army was understandably going to be less-than-hospitable to the attackers. They would throw heavy objects, shoot sharp objects, and pour hot liquids from above as the soldiers were trying to scale the wall. How rude!

For an epic visual of what that might look like think of the Battle of Helm's Deep in the movie The Lord of the Rings: The Two Towers. Lots of costs. Lots of casualties.

If the cost-benefit analysis prevailed and time allowed, a second strategy would be much more appealing. It was called a siege. Any number of old, low-budget Biblical-era action movies have likely given you a measure of familiarity with the siege.

As an alternative to an immediate attack, a king could deploy his army to surround a city. They would cut off all entry and exit from the city. Since many ancient cities were built on waterways for obvious reasons, often an army would divert the life-giving liquid around the city so there would be no food or water available for the inhabitants. Then the attacking king would send a message

13

to the city's leadership and say, in essence, "Hey folks, we're not going to let any food in and we're not going to let any water in. And, by the way, we're not letting any people or products out. We are just going to be out here hanging around with our food and drink and comforts. As soon as you 'know when to fold'em' let us know and we will be ready to accept your surrender."

And that is basically what happened in II Kings 6. And the situation became severe. The siege led to a famine.

*There was a great famine in the city; the siege lasted so long that a donkey's head sold for eighty shekels of silver, and a quarter of a cab of seed pods for five shekels. (II Kings 6:25)*

The famine got worse and worse and worse to the point where they were eating things that were reasonably unthinkable to us. First, we are told that they were eating donkey heads. That's bad enough. This next phrase is difficult to translate from the original language but let me tell you what respected scholars say that they were eating, (I'll try to say this delicately): dove dung, pigeon poop. Got the picture?

I've been to over 60 countries all around the world. I have eaten things that were simply unappetizing and things that were supremely disgusting. I draw the line at things that are moving. From a speaker many years ago at the Urbana Missions Conference that is sponsored by Intervarsity, I learned a prayer that I have used on five continents: "Lord, I will eat it all up, if you will keep it all down!"

I've been extraordinarily hungry at various times in my life. But never once, I can tell you assuredly, have I ever wanted to eat a donkey head. And I never have… that I know of, at least. And I've certainly not wanted to eat pigeon poop.

But the residents of Samaria were eating these things, and you say to yourself, "Oh my goodness, could it ever get worse than that? Is there any possible chance that the famish of the famine progresses to the point where it is more shocking than eating those kinds of things?"

And the answer is yes!

It got much, much worse. The passage continues:

*As the king of Israel was passing by on the wall, a woman cried to him, "Help me, my lord the king!" The king replied, "If the LORD does not help you, where can I get help for you? From the threshing floor? From the winepress?" Then he asked her, "What's the matter?" (II Kings 6:26-28)*

We meet a woman who came to the king as he was walking on top of the wall of the city. Maybe he was looking at the armies arrayed against him outside the wall and looking at the starvation staring at him from inside the wall. Whatever he was thinking, he certainly was not exuding confidence in the crisis.

The desperate woman asks for help and the king basically replies that there is none available if she is looking for food or drink: "God help you because I can't." But she was not exactly looking for food. At least not directly.

*She answered, "This woman said to me, 'Give up your son so that we may eat him today, and tomorrow we'll eat my son.' So, we cooked my son and ate him. The next day I said to her, 'Give up your son so that we may eat him,' but she had hidden him." (II Kings 6:28-29)*

Do you catch the gravity of the famine? This woman pleads, "Listen, King, I want you to referee a dispute I have with this woman here next to me." And he replies, "OK what's going on

15

ladies?" "The starvation is severe, and we are desperate, so yesterday we made a deal, we made a pact, we signed a covenant that we were going to eat my son one day and the next day we were going to eat her son." The petitioner complains that although they had cannibalized her son, the other mother was in breach of contract because she was hiding her son so they could not eat him.

Can you imagine the awful situation where people have decided that for their own appetites, for their own survival, for their own comfort, they're going to sacrifice their own children? That is how awful the situation got.

And that is the context in which we are introduced to four men when we fast-forward a couple of verses into chapter 7.

*Now there were four men with leprosy at the entrance of the city gate. (II Kings 7:3)*

We meet four men. They were not only suffering from a serious deprivation: food and drink, they were also suffering from a serious disease: leprosy. They were waiting outside the city gate because leprosy at that time was an incurable disease, a progressive disease, a highly transmittable disease, and a quarantining disease. A person with this illness, according to Leviticus 13 was required to *"wear torn clothes, let his hair be unkempt, cover the lower part of his face and cry out, 'Unclean! Unclean!' and must live alone and outside the camp." (Leviticus 13:45-46)*

So, these men with leprosy were stuck just outside the city gate. They couldn't go into the city because of the law and the famine. They couldn't go out to the fields because of the hostile army. So, they parked themselves at the gate while the famine raged, and the army waited. But their parking permit expired.

16

*They said to each other, "Why stay here until we die? If we say, 'We'll go into the city' – the famine is there, and we will die. And if we stay here, we will die. So let's go over to the camp of the Arameans and surrender. If they spare us, we live; if they kill us, then we die." (II Kings 7:3-4)*

They realistically discerned their dilemma. They said to themselves, "Listen if we stay here, we die because there's no food here. If we go into the city, we die because the famine is there. If we go out into the surrounding armies, we'll probably die, but they have food and at least they may fill us before they kill us."

And so, they made a courageous decision. To be saved they must make a move. They decided to go out to the surrounding armies. And look what happened:

*At dusk they got up and went to the camp of the Arameans. When they reached the edge of the camp, no one was there for the Lord had caused the Arameans to hear the sound of chariots and horses and a great army, so that they said to one another, "Look, the king of Israel has hired the Hittite and Egyptian kings to attack us!" So they got up and fled in the dusk and abandoned their tents and their horses and donkeys. They left the camp as it was and ran for their lives. (II Kings 7:5-7)*

Do you see what has happened? Moments before, these men were hopelessly and helplessly sitting at the gate of the city realizing that there was nothing they could do to save themselves. They were dead if they stayed, they were dead if they went in, they were dead if they went out, and they had no hope whatsoever.

They made a choice. They got up and moved. And they found that God had done a miracle.

God confounded the minds of the Aramean army and, believing that they were under attack, they raced off leaving everything they had to be found by the four despairing lepers.

*The men who had leprosy reached the edge of the camp, entered one of the tents and ate and drank. Then they took silver, gold and clothes, and went off and hid them. They returned and entered another tent and took some things from it and hid them also. (II Kings 7:7-8)*

Here are four guys who moments before were helpless, hopeless, dead if they stayed, dead if they went, dead if they did nothing, and dead if they did something unless God intervened. Then God did.

And because of a miracle, in the blink of an eye, they received blessings beyond their wildest dreams. They had all the food they needed and wanted and more. They had all the drink they needed and wanted and more. They had all the wealth they needed and wanted and more. They had all the clothing they needed and wanted and more.

They gorged themselves on the foodstuffs. They dressed in a red-carpet-worthy wardrobe. They stuffed their pockets with riches.

Then they thought of the future. They reasoned that they should fund their retirement plan. They didn't have time to build bigger barns, so in the post-dusk darkness, they hauled the bounty up into the surrounding hillside and hid it for the future. They were set! They had everything they could ever imagine for now and the future, not because of their own work or wit but because of the unmerited miracle of God.

And then something happens!

Something happens that should lay hold of our hearts faster than the four men laid hold of the loot.

*Then they said to each other, "We're not doing right. This is a day of good news, and we are keeping it to ourselves. If we wait till daylight, punishment will overtake us. Let's go at once and report this to the royal palace." (II Kings 7:9)*

They came to their senses. Suddenly, in the blissful moment, while observing and enjoying the incredible blessings that God had bestowed on them, they realized that the blessings they enjoyed in abundance were available to save those in the city as well. But the people in the city were unreached with the good news. The people in the city were dying without ever hearing the message that salvation was available to them.

And the men knew that it was just not right to withhold the message that will save from the multitude who won't survive.

Let me say it again; it is just not right to withhold the message that will save from the multitude who won't survive.

It doesn't take a literary scholar to see the parallel between these four men and those of us who are Christians, does it? We who are believers and who have stepped over the line of faith in Jesus Christ have been taken from death and showered with blessings unimaginable. The Bible says that before we came to faith in Jesus Christ we were "dead in our trespasses and sins." We could do nothing to save ourselves. We were dead if we stayed where we were, dead if we moved somewhere else, dead if we did nothing, and dead if we tried something.

It should not surprise you that the Apostle Paul says it better than I ever could:

19

*As for you, you were dead in your transgressions and sins, in which you used to live when you followed the ways of this world and of the ruler of the kingdom of the air, the spirit who is now at work in those who are disobedient. All of us also lived among them at one time, gratifying the cravings of our flesh and following its desires and thoughts. Like the rest, we were by nature deserving of wrath. But because of his great love for us, God, who is rich in mercy, made us alive with Christ even when we were dead in transgressions – it is by grace you have been saved. And God raised us up with Christ and seated us with him in the heavenly realms in Christ Jesus, in order that in the coming ages he might show the incomparable riches of his grace, expressed in his kindness to us in Christ Jesus. For it is by grace you have been saved, through faith – and this is not from yourselves, it is the gift of God not by works, so that no one can boast. (Ephesians 2:1-9)*

God did a miracle on the cross that was infinitely more miraculous than confusing Arameans or providing earthly riches. Jesus Christ died for us. By faith, we can come into a relationship with him and at that moment we are saved and, with salvation, showered with not donkeys and horses and riches and clothes, but with incredible spiritual blessings: forgiveness of all of our sins, eternal life promised with Christ in heaven, the church as a family here on earth, the Bible to guide us, the Holy Spirit to live inside of us, total reconciliation with God and a relationship with him and so, so, so much more.

Blessing upon blessing upon blessing. And yet, do you know what I see happening? All around our world, I see people who, like the lepers of II Kings, have absorbed those blessings, enjoyed those blessings, and understood that they have those blessings for eternity and that their future is secured... but, for any number of reasons, their mind never considers the people they just left in the darkness of hopelessness and who've never heard that salvation and those blessings are freely and bountifully available simply for the faith-asking.

Those of us who have experienced God's miraculous salvation must share it with the unreached in darkness. It is simply the right thing to do!

# Chapter - 3
# THE HONOR OF BEING GOD'S AMBASSADOR

My wedding ring has not been removed from my finger in over 40 years. And it will not be any time soon. Medically speaking, it is because I have bony enlargements occurring at the proximal interphalangeal joints. In layman's terms, that means that the knuckles have gotten bigger in the middle joints of my fingers while the ring, unsurprisingly, has stayed the same size.

Just as my marriage is permanent, my wedding ring is now permanent, too. It will not come off my finger without someone cutting off either the ring or the finger. If it ever must be removed while I am alive, I have a preference for which one they should cut.

Since the ring cannot be removed, you are just going to have to take my word for this: Inscribed on the inside of my ring is a scripture reference that my wife and I aspirationally chose to represent our marriage.

*For Christ's love compels us, because we are convinced that one died for all, and therefore all died. And he died for all, that those who live should no longer live for themselves but for him who died for them and was raised again. (II Corinthians 5:14-15)*

Our deep desire was that we, like Paul who wrote those words, would be so filled with the love of Christ that it would overflow into our relationship with him, with each other, and with others. With much imperfection, we have sought to make that true for over four decades.

My old King James Version Bible renders that verse, "*For the love of Christ constrains us.*" The Greek word translated as *compel* or *constrain* is interesting. "Sunecho" is a compound word from *sun*, meaning with or together and *echo*, meaning to hold or possess.

Strong literally translates "sunecho" as to hold together or compress.

When I think of this concept my mind goes back to an experience I had in an Asian airport a decade ago. I was flying on my way home from Colombo, Sri Lanka. For reasons I will not explain but which had everything to do with getting the cheapest flights, the routing for my return trip to the United States took me from Colombo to Singapore to Jakarta to Tokyo to New York.

The length of time from my first "wheels up" to the last landing was about 35 hours. Add that to the fact that I left Colombo in the late evening after having been awake all day and the fact that I don't sleep on airplanes due to my 6'4" frame not quite fitting into the cheap seats where I fly in the back of the plane. You can imagine the slight grogginess that descended on me as I prepared to board the fourth leg of the trip at Tokyo's Narita Airport.

When the gate agent called our flight, a 747 Jumbo, I and about 500 of my closest friends stood and moved toward the gangway. I'm not sure of the cultural reasoning but personal space in that environment was pretty much nonexistent.

Parenthetically and somewhat humorously, as the huge crowd pressed into me, I opened my eyes, looked around, and saw a sea of heads with thick, black hair about 5'6" above the ground with only my tall, bald, white dome poking out from the masses. It reminded me of a flight I had taken a few months before from Nairobi, Kenya to Dar es Salaam, Tanzania. As we cruised at about 30,000 feet, there was a thick, flat cloud cover as far as the eye could see with the only break being the tall, white snow-covered top of Mount Kilimanjaro protruding out above the clouds. Just call me Kilimanjaro.

Back to Tokyo. As the crowd pressed in and held or constrained me, the gate opened and without effort, and some what without my will, I was moved along by the force of the crowd. The mass of humanity did a "sunecho" on me. It held me fast, compressed me, constrained me, and compelled me to move where it wanted.

Although he could not have imagined trans-Pacific air travel or Asian airports, it seems that this is the image that the apostle Paul wants his readers to picture when they consider his motivation for ministry. He implies that there was something outside of him, something that pressed him forward almost without effort and almost without his will, something that constrained him and compelled him onward.

What was that "something?" It was the LOVE of God. *"For Christ's love compels us..."*

Why did Paul share the Good News with those who have never heard of it? In large part, because he had experienced God's love in such a compelling way that it moved him to respond; that it moved him to action; that it moved him to accept God's Great Commission to represent him to other people who were loved by God yet were looking for love in all the wrong places. The hurting people were aliens to God's love and strangers to God's kingdom.

24

Paul had, as a result of having responded to God's loving offer, received a new relationship with God and, with it, innumerable blessings. He says, *"All this is from God, who reconciled us to himself through Christ" (II Corinthians 5:18a).* In the process of reconciliation in Christ, God changed Paul's standing from that of being separated from him to that of being his beloved child. How could he do that? He tells us a few verses later.

*God made him [Jesus] who had no sin to be sin for us so that we might become the righteousness of God in him. (II Corinthians 5:21)*

It is the Great Exchange! Jesus who never sinned, takes off his pure, white garment and holds it out to me. He exchanges it for my filthy, stained, disgusting, smelly, blood-soaked shirt, and the backpack of weighty sin that comes with it. He takes my sinfulness with its deserved penalty, and I get his righteousness with its deserved reward.

OK, let's stop here for a moment.
Don't just blow by this.
Ponder.

Let this truth soak into your mind and heart until the inexplicable wonder overtakes you. If you need to, lay down this book, close your eyes, and contemplate deeply on that.

How do you feel when you fully understand the love that led to the Great Exchange? What would you do for someone who would do that for you? You'd do anything he wants!

What does he want? He tells us what he wants.

*"All this is from God, who reconciled us to himself through Christ and gave us the ministry of reconciliation: that God was reconciling the world to himself in Christ, not counting mankind's sin against them. And he has committed to us the message of*

*reconciliation. We are therefore Christ's ambassadors as though God were making his appeal through us. We implore you on Christ's behalf: be reconciled to God." (I Corinthians 5:18-20)*

Because of what God has done in us, and because he has commissioned us with a message of reconciliation, we are God's ambassadors.

What is an ambassador?

An ambassador is a citizen of one country who is living in another country, taking the message of the leadership of their home country to the people of the country in which they reside.

Jessica Brodie helpfully notes, "For early Christian readers, an 'ambassador' was someone who represented one state or land to another. They were official representatives of the one who sent them and were therefore to be treated with the utmost respect. It was a well-known title, one that carried a great deal of respect and dignity, and that warranted great decorum on the part of the ambassador, the sender, and the receiver. By 'ambassadors of Christ,' Paul meant that Christians should see themselves as representatives of God - and were to behave accordingly. They had an important job to do showcase Christ, and deliver His message so others could know Him, too."

If you have responded to the compelling love of God and come to faith in Jesus Christ, then you are a citizen of God's kingdom, and as his subject, God has appointed or commissioned you as his Royal Ambassador, his representative.

God says, "I have a message to share with all the people in the location in which you live (earth). And that message is the message of reconciliation. The message is that by faith in the work of my son Jesus on their behalf, the people to whom I send you can receive eternal life and be rightly related to me."

The ambassador's appointment carries with it the certainty of a corresponding obligation. Arrestingly, it also carries the possibility of a resulting ordeal. As he sits in prison for proclaiming the message of reconciliation, the Apostle Paul pleads with his dear friends in Ephesus:

*"Pray also for me, that whenever I open my mouth, words may be given me so that I will fearlessly make known the mystery of the gospel, for which I am an ambassador in chains. Pray that I may declare it fearlessly as I should [as is necessary and proper given the honor of my appointment]." (Ephesians 6:19-20)*

And it is an extraordinary honor to be a representative of the living God. It is an honor to be an ambassador.

If my nation's leadership were to call me and say, "Jack, we know you've been to a lot of countries, and we know you have a real heart for the people of those countries. We'd like for you to be the U.S. Ambassador to one of those countries." It would be a mark of respect to be chosen to do that and a privilege to represent my country and all my fellow citizens. That would be a wonderful honor.

But I would have to turn it down. I'd have to tell them "I've already accepted an Ambassadorship, sorry. I'm doing it for a different ruler."

My King, Jesus, has appointed me (and each who follows him) to be his Ambassador to All Nations. In response to that greater honor, I want to faithfully do my part to fulfill my charge to bring his message to the world in which I temporarily reside. How about you?

27

# Chapter - 4
# THE REALITY OF HELL

In Luke chapter 16 Jesus tells a very familiar story to make a very clear point.

*"There was a rich man who was dressed in purple and fine linen and lived in luxury every day. At his gate was laid a beggar named Lazarus, covered with sores and longing to eat what fell from the rich man's table. Even the dogs came and licked his sores.*

*"The time came when the beggar died and the angels carried him to Abraham's side. The rich man also died and was buried. In hell, where he was in torment, he looked up and saw Abraham far away, with Lazarus by his side. So he called to him, 'Father Abraham, have pity on me and send Lazarus to dip the tip of his finger in water and cool my tongue, because I am in agony in this fire.'*

*"But Abraham replied, 'Son, remember that in your lifetime you received your good things, while Lazarus received bad things, but now he is comforted here and you are in agony. And besides all this, between us and you a great chasm has been set in place so that those who want to go from here to you cannot, nor can anyone cross over from there to us.'*

*"He answered, 'Then I beg you, Father, send Lazarus to my family, for I have five brothers. Let him warn them so that they*

*will not also come to this place of torment.' Abraham replied,*
*'They have Moses and the Prophets; let them listen to them.'*

*"'No, Father Abraham,' he said, 'but if someone from the*
*dead goes to them, they will repent.' He said to him, 'If they do*
*not listen to Moses and the Prophets, they will not be convinced*
*even if someone rises from the dead.'" (Luke 16:19-31 NIV)*

Before we take a closer look at the cast of characters Jesus
introduced in this narrative let's take a quick look at the context.

Earlier in this chapter, Jesus told his disciples: *"There was a*
*rich man whose manager was accused of wasting his*
*possessions…" (Luke 16:1).*

Later, he comments, *"No man can serve two masters. Either*
*he will hate the one and love the other, or he will be devoted to*
*the one and despise the other. You cannot serve both God and*
*money." (Luke 16:13)*

*"The Pharisees, who loved money, heard all this, and were*
*sneering at Jesus. He said to them…" (Luke 16:14)*

Jesus indicates that a person cannot trust and be devoted to
"Mammon" and God. The Aramaic word translated mammon
means riches, possessions, money, or property. It may have been
related to the Hebrew word AMAN meaning to trust. Here, Jesus
is unambiguous that a person cannot trust/serve God and trust/
serve something else. Yet, with transparent and convicted hearts,
we ask ourselves how often we profess that we trust God, and
call him our master, and yet belie that profession by holding, even
hoarding, wealth for our own enjoyment, and our own perceived
security.

I asked myself whether Luke could look at me and describe
me as, "Jack, who loves money (possessions, property, purchasing

power)?" That's not the target of this chapter... And it's a bit convicting, so let's move on.

At the mention of the inability to serve God and money, the Pharisees sneered. Why? Likely, they were a product of their culture and their religious training. Their culture and religious sensitivities saw riches as the logical result of righteousness. To them, if you do good, then you and your family and your nation are blessed by God, and you get to live your best life now. If you fall short, then you get cursed and "no soup for you."

It's what John Lynch describes as "The Santa Claus is Coming to Town Theology."

He relates that as early as we can remember, we perform for acceptance. If we are good enough, talented enough, together enough, beautiful enough, right and correct enough, then we will be loved, accepted, blessed, and happy. And, if not, we will be rejected and receive a lousy life.

It's reflected in the song that Frances Coots and Haven Gillespie wrote to be performed first in 1934:

You better watch out. You better not cry. You better not pout. I'm telling you why; Santa Claus is coming to town. He's making a list, checking it twice, going to find out who's naughty or nice. Santa Claus is coming to town. He knows when you're sleeping. He knows when you're awake. He knows if you've been bad or good. So be good for goodness' sake.

There it is. If you're good, you get good things and if you aren't, you get bad things. The culture sings it, and they believe it.

That noxious theology says that someone is watching from on high, and your value is based on how much you do right and how little you do wrong. And this guy is constantly writing down the wrong you have done so that he can bring it up against you at a future time. And if you're naughty; no presents for you, only coal in your stocking.

And he's going to find you out. This omniscient, controlling legalist has got the list and he's coming to town! So, you better watch out. You better fear this guy. You better stop your whining and sniveling. You better not pout. You better put on a good face. You're constantly on trial and if you want good things to happen in your life, you had best figure out how to keep this guy pleased.

The Pharisees did not have that song or Lynch's analysis, but they had that theology. And, sadly, so do many people in our age.

So, to a Pharisee, and too many who thought like them in the first century and think like them in our century, a rich person would obviously have the inside track to God, and to Heaven. They must've been good, for goodness' sake.

As CI Scofield notes, "to the Jewish people temporal prosperity was a token of divine favor." Just as it is possible to grab a verse and build an erroneous belief on it, a cursory reading of certain hand-picked passages of the Old Testament without a knowledge of the full sweep and scope of divine revelation could lead even a faithful person to that mistaken conclusion. When you have a free moment, give a quick read of Deuteronomy 28 and apply that passage immediately to yourself without proper interpretation practices and you can see how someone would come to that same conclusion.

I'm not going to go on a tangential rant on the appalling practice of ancient and modern people of trying to apply Scripture (what does this mean to me?) without interpreting it (what did this text means to the original hearers in its normal grammatical-historical contextual sense and compared with other Scripture). But I could rant if you want me to. Just give me a call. And remember, as I mentioned a few chapters ago, if you take a text out of context you are left with a con.

This erroneous evaluation of the bestowal of material blessing even led Jesus' disciples to have their heads explode when he commented on a rich young ruler who could not follow Jesus because he had great riches in which he trusted. Jesus said, *"It is easier for a camel to go through the eye of a needle than for a rich man to enter the kingdom of God." (Mark 10:25)*

The disciples' response? *"The disciples were even more amazed and said to each other, 'Who then can be saved?'" (Mark 10:26)*

Are you kidding, Jesus? Are you punking us? Where is the hidden camera, Allen Funt? (Google Allan Funt if you're under 50 and don't understand that reference).

The account of Jesus' interaction with the rich young ruler and disciples is also found in Luke 18. Two chapters before Jesus shocks them with the aforementioned camel analogy, the disciples, infected by their confused culture and misleading leaders, likely thought that rich men had heaven in the bag. Done deal. Forgone conclusion. No need to think about a rich guy not getting into heaven.

So, back to Luke 16. To the Pharisees (who loved the purchasing power) and disciples (whom we just described), Jesus introduces the characters of his short story. We are not sure if they are actual characters or simply used as an illustration. I'm tempted to think that this is the recounting of an actual story known to Jesus. However, I could be wrong. Why do I lean that way? First, it is not introduced as a parable (a teaching tool in which a spiritual/heavenly truth is illustrated by placing it alongside an easily understood earthly story) as most other parable portions are. Additionally, it uses a specific name (Lazarus) and that does not happen in any of Jesus' other over 40 recorded parables.

Parable or true story, the account Jesus told must have also left his hearers more than amazed.

The first person we meet in his narrative is a man who is described as a rich man. How rich was he? Let's note how he is described.

The word *rich* is derived from the word for *full* which is derived from the word for *abundance*. It has been described as "muchness." This man was abundantly supplied with the world's goods. He was full and had all that he needed and wanted.

We're told he is clothed in purple. Purple-died cloth is symbolic of royal status. He had a regal position, or at least a regal demeanor, as the ruler of his circumstances.

Along with his regal purple, he was clothed in fine linen. The word for linen, "byssos," describes a very expensive, very delicate, and very sought-after form of linen cloth made from a specific species of Egyptian flax. This guy had soft delicate clothes, as opposed to the rough and scratchy cheap garments of a John the Baptist, an average fisherman, or a poor beggar outside his gate.

Our passage tells us that he lived in luxury. The phrase "lived in luxury" is actually a singular Greek word: "euphraino." The prefix *eu* means good as in a eulogy is speaking good (eu) words (logos) or the gospel (*euangelion* in Greek) is the good (eu) news or message (*angelion*). The second part of the word is from *phren*,

33

which J. Thayer says is properly "the midriff (diaphragm); the parts around the heart" and figuratively the person's inward feelings, or mindset that regulates outward behavior.

In the case of our rich friend, he had a good inward feeling about his circumstances in life and therefore he rested and relaxed in luxury and celebratory partying.

And he did that *"every day."* The good life of this rich, pampered, regal man was not just an occasional night out. It was an everyday experience. In fact, every minute of every hour of every day of every week of every month of every year, this man lived the "good life."

Do you get the picture? The first cast member that Jesus brought to the stage was the poster child for Jewish blessedness. Now, for the other side of the spectrum.

In verse 20, we meet another man. The antithesis of the nameless rich man.

His name is Lazarus. Notice there is dignity bestowed upon him as he is given a name. He is not an unidentified form on the street. He has a name. His parents gave him a name. He is a person, a human, conceived with, and still retaining the image of God, even as he suffers in inexplicable indignity. His name is Lazarus.

Lazarus is described in virtually all English translations as either a poor man or a beggar. The literal translation of the Greek word used here is one who crouches or cowers. You can likely imagine why this word, over time, came to denote a poor beggar. In contrast to the regal, upright demeanor of the rich man, who partied daily and demanded prominent attention, Lazarus shrunk into the shadows and survived out of the limelight, and seemingly out of the attention of people or God.

Lazarus was covered with sores. His skin was pocked with ulcerated lesions and the implication was that he suffered from them every minute of every hour of every day of every week of every month of every year. Bodily pain was his constant companion.

Not only was Lazarus' visible body suffering, but his stomach also suffered as well as he longed (the word means coveted, lusted after, set his heart upon, truly yearned) for just the discarded scraps from the luxurious table of the rich man.

The word describes not a passive wish list occasionally referenced, but an intensely passionate and driven impulse. Lazarus was not just missing his afternoon tea and scone. He was starving, living chronically without nourishment.

As he slowly starved, likely to death, he weakly sat by the garbage pile outside the rich man's gated community waiting for the accumulated table scraps to be dumped into a pile to be gathered by the garbage collectors. There he competed with the pack of dogs which waited for the same sustenance. When the "food" was gone, the dogs would satisfy themselves by licking the fresh flesh on Lazarus, his legs, arms, and torso.

And then he died.

Before your Western-influenced mind protests that something like this could never happen today, let me tell you that it does. Follow me to the streets of any of 100 major cities in the majority world. Go home with my dear Indian friend and indigenous missionary colleague and meet the children whom he has rescued from trash piles in his city and in area villages. There are people like Lazarus living in misery all over the world today. But, Jesus did not tell us this story to draw attention to the misery of the poor man in life but to highlight the misery of the rich man after death.

Reread verses 22-24 and notice the "*in*" statements. The rich man who had been "*in purple*" and "*in luxury*" was now "*in hell*," "*in torment*," "*in agony*," and "*in the fire*." What a condition change!

This led the man who had lacked little and shared less in life to become the one who had an intensely passion-driven impulse for just a drop of water.

He who had shown no apparent pity in life begged for pity. He asked for Lazarus (whom we are told was transported in death to "Abraham's side") to cool his tormented tongue with just a drop of water. But heartbreakingly, it was not possible.

He suffered, fully conscious of his suffering. Contrary to what some would have us believe, and even what would be comforting to believe, this indicates that death is not a cessation of conscious existence. Those of us who are humans (which I would assume is most everyone reading these words) have an eternal existence that has already begun on earth and will continue for us after death. The most important question, perhaps the only important question is, "Where are we going to spend that eternal life?"

The rich man found himself in hell, craving relief from his torment. But the sad, sad reality is that no relief was going to come. No relief was possible.

As I write those words, I feel a physical reaction in my body. As you read them, what do you notice in yours?

Abraham, I believe with pain in his heart and a sigh on his lips, replies to the man's request for a water drop.

First, notice he calls him "*Son.*" It reminds me of John 8:12-47 where Pharisees opposed Jesus another time. In response to some of his teachings, they asserted, "*We are children of Abraham.*" Ultimately, Jesus retorts, "*If you were Abraham's children you would do the things Abraham did.*" Remember Abraham "*believed the LORD and it was accounted to him as righteousness*" *(Genesis 15:6).*

These people were physical descendants/sons of Abraham but as Paul says, "*Consider Abraham: 'He believed God, and it was credited to him as righteousness.' Understand, then, that those who believe are children of Abraham. The Scriptures foresaw that God would justify the Gentiles by faith, and announced the gospel in advance to Abraham: 'All nations will be blessed through you.' So those who have faith are blessed along with Abraham, the man of faith.*" *(Galatians 3:6-9)*

In another place, Jesus tells a particular group without faith in him, "*you belong to your father, the devil…*" *(John 8:44).*

You see, the rich man could be called Abraham's son by heredity, but he was not Abraham's son in faith. He did not do as Abraham did. He did not believe God's message and therefore found himself in hell.

This is the clear and unambiguous revelation of the Bible. Hell is a real place and real people go there. The equally clear and unambiguous revelation of the Bible is the key that opens the door to heaven is faith in the death, burial, and resurrection of Jesus Christ as the one who bore my sin, and acceptance of his offer of eternal life.

*For God, so loved the world that he gave his one and only son, that whoever believes in him shall not perish, but have eternal life. For God did not send his son into the world to condemn the world, but to save the world through him. Whoever believes in him is not condemned, but whoever does not believe stands condemned already, because he has not believed in the name of God's one and only son. (John 3:16-18)*

Whatever can be read into Abraham's conversation with the rich man, this is clear: the decision that determines destiny is made before death.

Abraham, sadly I believe, replies that *"...between us and you a great chasm has been fixed, so that those who want to go from here to you cannot, nor can anyone crossover from there to us."*

There is not a toll bridge between hell and heaven that can be traversed with prayerful requests, sacrificial offerings, good works, candle-filled rituals, or the pleadings of others. Nor is there any reincarnation that will give a person a chance to move up the food chain in a subsequent life.

Again, the decision that determines destiny is made before death.

Let me take a moment and digress. Remember that in the introduction to this book, I admitted that this book was aimed towards people who are believers in Jesus Christ; those who have made the decision to put their faith in Christ's sacrificial death for them because they know they cannot now, and never will be "good enough" to merit heaven? If you have read this far and are not among them, let me invite you, in the light of what you have read, to go to the appendix at the end of this book and read, understand, and respond to his offer of eternal life. If you have any questions about that, please contact me via Worldlink's website: www.worldlinkonline.org.

Back to Jesus' story.

So, we have two men who lived drastically different lives, died drastically different deaths, and experienced drastically different post-mortem existences. And I have brought you through all of that to get you to the next few verses.

In response to the now-settled realization of his eternal lost state, the formerly rich man, pleads, *"Then [because of what I now know about hell and the need to make an eternity-sealing choice before a person dies], I beg you, Father, send Lazarus to my father's house, for I have five brothers. Let him warn them so that they will not also come to this place of torment."*

Who is the beggar now?

He wanted for nothing on earth. But now he deeply and urgently begs for one thing; that the message that will save others be shared with them before it is too late.

Five minutes in hell turned a formerly self-absorbed and self-indulgent navel-gazer into a Great Commission Champion. The reality of hell will do that.

General William Booth, the founder of the Salvation Army, is quoted as having said, "most ministries would like their new recruits to have spent 4 to 5 years in seminary for theological training. I would prefer our new recruits spend five minutes in hell: that would be enough to prepare people for a lifetime of compassionate ministry."

# Chapter - 5
# THE JOY OF SEEING SOMEONE SAVED

It was Thursday, February 8, 2018. My wife, Nancy, and I donned our midnight green gear and hopped in our 2004 Toyota Camry to make our way to a friend's house, and then the train station. While walking the final blocks to the nearby train station we merged into a sea of similarly clad people.

While we rode the 30 minutes into downtown Philadelphia, songs would occasionally break forth from the passengers, and be immediately joined by hundreds of others in the train cars.

When we reached our final station and alighted near Center City, we were greeted by somewhere between 750,000 and 1,500,000 Philadelphia Eagles football fans. All were there to celebrate the Eagle's victory in the National Football League's Super Bowl LII (52). For those reading this in other countries, think Olympic gold medal winner, UEFA Champions League winner, English Premier League title celebration, tennis Grand Slam victory, or winning a green jacket at golf's Masters Tournament.

We made our way on to the Ben Franklin Parkway and claimed our roughly one square foot of space along with involuntarily jostling fans as far as the eye could see. When the football team finally arrived at the end of the 5-mile parade route, I cheered them on and watched the crowd scream their approval.

I saw deep happiness, maybe even joy. I know that we could argue whether it was temporal happiness, which would (and did) end shortly thereafter. But for the moment, I saw, and to a degree felt, an emotional release that brought pleasure as I and a million of my then-closest friends enjoyed something that had been elusive to the team and, for the moment, was important to us.

But it was not of ultimate importance.

In an interview in *Psychology Today*, Pamela Ebstyne King, Ph.D., talks about joy as opposed to happiness. Dr. King is the Peter L. Benson Associate Professor of Applied Developmental Science at the Thrive Center for Human Development in the School of Psychology at Fuller Theological Seminary. That is a mouthful, but basically means that she has studied and thought of these things quite deeply.

She opines, "I have observed that many people have an enduring and underlying sense of something that is deeper than the emotion of happiness, and I have come to describe this as joy. In my study of joy, I have also noticed that joy is more complex than a feeling or an emotion. It is something one can practice, cultivate, or make a habit. Consequently, I suggest that joy is most fully understood as a virtue that involves our thoughts, feelings, and actions in response to what matters most in our lives. Thus, joy is an enduring, deep delight in what holds the most significance."

Let me highlight that last sentence again; "Thus, joy is an enduring, deep delight in what holds the most significance."

Jesus describes a situation where we see "an enduring, deep delight in what holds the most significance." We find the account reported in Luke 15 where Jesus offers three parables, easy-to-understand earthly stories that have deep spiritual lessons.

When I study parables, I like to look at 4 things; the Situation (context), the Illustration (what was said), the Explanation (what it means), and the Application (what it means for my life). So, let's do that.

## THE SITUATION

*Now the tax collectors and sinners were all gathering around to hear Jesus. But the Pharisees and the teachers of the law muttered, "This man welcomes sinners, and eats with them." (Luke 15:1-2)*

Jesus was heading toward Jerusalem, where he would make his final loving sacrifice of his life for the sins of the whole world. Luke 14:25 tells us that *"large crowds were traveling with Jesus."* He loved each and every one of them. He wanted to be with each and every one of them; the "best" and the "worst". Those that adhered to religion and those that abhorred religion. He would welcome each and every one of them to be with him and to hear his message, and hopefully turn from their chosen path of sin, to come back to the one who truly valued them. He was about to die for their salvation. Each and every one of them.

But not everyone felt that way. A group of religious know-it-alls knew nothing of God's heart for the broken people who were converging on Jesus, longing to hear his message.

This gathering was just what Jesus wanted. Because of their inestimable value to him, he longed for the hurting people to come and hear him, and then to act on what they heard by turning from whatever they were trusting as of ultimate importance and turning to God.

But the Pharisees and teachers of the law muttered. The Greek word translated muttered, is an onomatopoeia; a word that sounds like what it describes. In this case, it sounds like buzzing bees. Non descript, annoying, incessant murmuring. The self-righteous mutterers thought that God surely did not want these "sinners" near him and if this Jesus knew God half as well as they did, he wouldn't want them near him either.

Those who were far from God and knew it were gathering. Those who were far from God and didn't know it were grumbling.

So, Jesus tells them three stories to encourage them both to understand God's heart for those who are unreached with the message of his love and who are far away from him.

## THE ILLUSTRATION

It is a long passage from Luke 15:3-24 but hang in there. Each section echoes the same message.

*Then Jesus told them this parable: "Suppose one of you has a hundred sheep and loses one of them. Doesn't he leave the ninety-nine in the open country and go after the lost sheep until he finds it? And when he finds it, he joyfully puts it on his shoulders and goes home. Then he calls his friends and neighbors together and says, 'Rejoice with me; I have found my lost sheep.' I tell you that in the same way there will be more rejoicing in heaven over one sinner who repents than over ninety-nine righteous people who do not need to repent.*

*"Or suppose a woman has ten silver coins and loses one. Doesn't she light a lamp, sweep the house and search carefully until she finds it? And when she finds it, she calls her friends*

*and neighbors together and says, 'Rejoice with me; I have found my lost coin.' In the same way, I tell you, there is rejoicing in the presence of the angels of God over one sinner who repents.*

*Jesus continued: "There was a man who had two sons. The younger one said to his father, 'Father, give me my share of the estate.' So he divided his property between them.*

*"Not long after that, the younger son got together all he had, set off for a distant country and there squandered his wealth in wild living. After he had spent everything, there was a severe famine in that whole country, and he began to be in need. So he went and hired himself out to a citizen of that country, who sent him to his fields to feed pigs. He longed to fill his stomach with the pods that the pigs were eating, but no one gave him anything.*

*"When he came to his senses, he said, 'How many of my father's hired servants have food to spare, and here I am starving to death! I will set out and go back to my father and say to him: Father, I have sinned against heaven and against you. I am no longer worthy to be called your son; make me like one of your hired servants.' So he got up and went to his father.*

*"But while he was still a long way off, his father saw him and was filled with compassion for him; he ran to his son, threw his arms around him and kissed him.*

*"The son said to him, 'Father, I have sinned against heaven and against you. I am no longer worthy to be called your son.'*

*"But the father said to his servants, 'Quick! Bring the best robe and put it on him. Put a ring on his finger and sandals on his feet. Bring the fattened calf and kill it. Let's have a feast and celebrate. For this son of mine was dead and is alive again; he was lost and is found.' So they began to celebrate."*

44

## THE EXPLANATION

Here are three similar situations of things lost and then found and the response of the finder. A lost sheep, a lost coin and a lost son. A seeking shepherd, a seeking woman, and a seeking father. A returned sheep, a returned coin, and a returned son. A rejoicing shepherd, a rejoicing woman, and a rejoicing father.

In the Bible, repetition is used for emphasis. Notice this repetition.

*"I tell you that in the same way there will be more rejoicing in heaven, over one sinner who repents than over 99 righteous persons who do not need to repent." (Luke 15:7)*

*"In the same way, I tell you, there is rejoicing in the presence of the angels of God, over one sinner who repents." (Luke 15:10)*

After a discussion about the attitude of the prodigal son's older brother, Jesus describes the rejoicing father's justification for his joy. *"But we had to celebrate and be glad, this brother of yours was dead, and is alive again; he was lost and is found." (Luke 15:32)*

If Pamela Ebstyne King is right and joy is a deep delight in what holds the most significance, then this must be the ultimate joy that followed the return of that which was ultimately valuable.

So, Jesus reveals (if they can understand his clear parable) to a group of grumbling religionists (and perhaps to a group of "sinners" who wondered why this Rabbi would hang out with them) that there is a party-worthy joy that results when one who is spiritually lost is found.

## THE APPLICATION

I am not sure that I need to spend much time applying this passage. The meaning seems quite clear.

All the hosts of heaven rejoice when one person comes to faith in Jesus, is forgiven of their sins, and is therefore reconciled (found and brought back together) with God. And they rejoice more for this than anything else. Why such immense rejoicing? Because of the immense significance of the souls of those who were lost but now are found.

So, the logical question is: what is the level of my rejoicing when I see or hear of unreached people coming into a relationship with Jesus?

During those times, when I have a God-inspired and rightly-ordered view of what holds the most significance in life, I find that my rejoicing makes a Super Bowl celebration pale by comparison. A million cheering fans can't compare with billions of heavenly fans roaring with joy as there is rejoicing in the presence of the angels of God over one sinner who repents.

I don't know about you, but I want more of that joy.

# Chapter - 6
# THE GLORY OF GOD

It was time to get intentional. It was time for a church to step up and God was making the call to a particular church. The account of that call is given in the Bible's New Testament history book called the Book of Acts.

The historical narrative of Jesus' birth, life, teaching, rejection, death, resurrection, and ascension is chronicled in the "Gospels" known as Matthew, Mark, Luke, and John. The book of Acts accepts the historical baton and carries the narrative forward with selective and important details of the ensuing years of the growth of the new and expanding called-out-group of believers in Jesus Christ.

A rough outline of the book can be seen in Acts 1:8. There Jesus, about 40 days after his resurrection and just before his ascension, tells his followers, *"But you will receive power when the Holy Spirit comes on you; and you will be my witnesses in Jerusalem, and in all Judea and Samaria, and to the ends of the earth."*

The second chapter of Acts begins the spread of the Good News in Jerusalem. On the day of Pentecost, the Holy Spirit inspires the radical declaration of the *"wonders of God" (Acts 2:11).* For the next six chapters, the message of salvation through the risen Christ seems loosely confined to Jerusalem.

By chapter 6, we read, *"so the word of God spread. The number of disciples in Jerusalem multiplied rapidly, and a large number of priests became obedient to the faith" (Acts 6:7)*. This eruption of faith is followed by an eruption of opposition.

The inevitable persecution of the new followers of "The Way" of Jesus, which begins in chapter 4, finds a face to be its first victim, and a face to be its first leader, near the end of chapter 7.

The first victim was Stephen. A man full of the Holy Spirit, wisdom, grace, and power, Stephen gave witness to the Good News of Jesus and exposed both people's guilt and God's grace. The guilt part enraged the Jewish leaders who heard it, and they killed him.

It is both interesting and instructive that the Greek word that is translated as "witness" in Acts 1:8, where Jesus said, "you will be my witnesses," is the Greek word "martyres," which has come to mean one who is killed for their witness. Stephen was the first Christian martyr recorded in the Bible.

Stephen's martyrdom did not make him a hero, it showed he already was one.

As Stephen is murdered for his faithful witness to Jesus, we meet a man named Saul of Tarsus. Acts 8:1 tells us that he stood nearby and *"was giving approval to his death."*

*On that day a great persecution broke out against the church in Jerusalem, and all except the apostles were scattered throughout Judea and Samaria. Godly men buried Stephen and mourned deeply for him. But Saul began to destroy the church. Going from house to house, he dragged off both men and women and put them in prison. (Acts 8:1b-3)*

The death of Stephen did not stop the longing of Christians for unreached people to know Christ, and it did not satisfy the lust for murderous restrictions by those who opposed him.

Saul meant it for evil, but God meant it for good.

*Those who had been scattered preached the word wherever they went. Philip went down to a city in Samaria and proclaimed the Messiah there. When the crowds heard Philip and saw the signs he performed, they all paid close attention to what he said... So there was great joy in that city. (Acts 8:4-5, 8)*

The believers were now witnesses in Judea and Samaria along with Jerusalem. Phase II of the Acts 1:8 outline was underway. God was spreading the Good News and Saul was spreading the bad blood. Then a funny thing happened on the way to Damascus.

*Meanwhile, Saul was still breathing out murderous threats against the Lord's disciples. He went to the high priest and asked him for letters to the synagogues in Damascus, so that if he found any there who belonged to the Way, whether men or women, he might take them as prisoners to Jerusalem. As he neared Damascus on his journey, suddenly a light from heaven flashed around him. He fell to the ground and heard a voice say to him, "Saul, Saul, why do you persecute me?"*

*"Who are you, Lord?" Saul asked.*

*"I am Jesus, whom you are persecuting," he replied. "Now get up and go into the city, and you will be told what you must do." (Acts 9:1-6)*

The miraculous conversion of Saul from a persecutor of Christians to a preacher of Christ is the subject of uncounted books and articles, and I will not recount them here. Suffice it to say, he was changed entirely, and after some brief sojourning in Jerusalem, Saul went back to his hometown of Tarsus (and the surrounding area) where God prepared him to be a choice servant for missionary ministry.

During this time, Christians had a measure of peace, while the Christian movement had a measure of success, spreading in Judea, Samaria, and beyond.

By the time we get to Acts chapter 11, Luke, the physician and historian, records:

*Now those who had been scattered by the persecution that broke out when Stephen was killed traveled as far as Phoenicia, Cyprus and Antioch, spreading the word only among Jews. Some of them, however, men from Cyprus and Cyrene, went to Antioch and began to speak to Greeks also, telling them the good news about the Lord Jesus. The Lord's hand was with them, and a great number of people believed and turned to the Lord.*

*News of this reached the church in Jerusalem, and they sent Barnabas to Antioch. When he arrived and saw what the grace of God had done, he was glad and encouraged them all to remain true to the Lord with all their hearts. He was a good man, full of the Holy Spirit and faith, and a great number of people were brought to the Lord.*

*Then Barnabas went to Tarsus to look for Saul, and when he found him, he brought him to Antioch. So for a whole year Barnabas and Saul met with the church and taught great numbers of people. The disciples were called Christians first at Antioch. (Acts 11:19-26)*

So, we see the first two phases of the Acts outline well underway (Jerusalem, Judea/Samaria) and a fledgling church in

Antioch, and a few further inroads into the rest of the world. But God has a missionary heart, and that good beginning was not good enough for the good news to spread to the whole world.

Jesus had died for the whole world. Jesus had commanded that disciples should be made from the whole world. How was God going to move his people out of their local area into the whole world? To whom was He going to give the next Spirit-led nudge toward the "uttermost parts of the earth?" And when would they be open to hearing about Phase III?

We see the answer in Acts chapter 13 as God chooses to visit the Antioch church and their recognized leaders. *"In the church at Antioch. There were prophets and teachers: Barnabas, Simeon called Niger, Lucius of Cyrene, Manaen (who had been brought up with Herod the tetrarch) and Saul." (Acts 13:1)*

These five men were recognized as the gifted leadership team of one of the most influential churches of the Bible's New Testament. They could not have been more different, yet perhaps they could not have been more alike.

Barnabas, a Cyprian Jew, whose given name was Joseph, (see Acts 4:36 and following) earned the nickname Barnabas, which means Son of Encouragement.

Simeon, called Niger, perhaps was given that moniker to distinguish him from other Simons and Simeons. The proper noun Niger was of Latin origin and the word simply meant black. Perhaps he was of Sub-Saharan African descent showing the rich diversity of leadership in this early church.

Lucius was from Cyrene which was the capital of a Roman province in Northern Africa (modern-day Libya). Some have speculated that Jews from this prosperous North African city migrated to Jerusalem in sufficient numbers to start their own synagogue (see Acts 6:8-9) and that some of them, having come to faith in Jesus, were part of the dispersion after the persecution of Acts chapters 7 and 8.

Manaen was a close associate of Herod the Tetrarch. The Greek word used to describe his upbringing with Herod is "*syntrophos.*" The prefix "syn" means the same or together (like synonyms are words that share the same meaning or synergy refers to two agents working together for a greater effect, or synchronized indicates happening at the same chronos or time). The second part of the word "*trophos*" is a word that simply means to feed, nourish, or nurse. Luke's use of this word indicates his understanding that these two were so closely raised that they were nourished/nursed by the same person. This is not an indication of the same mother, but more likely an indication of the same household and perhaps the same wet nurse. In any case, he was raised as a Greek, in likely a rich and powerful home.

Saul, who had been beckoned to Antioch by Barnabas to help the new church, was the last of the leaders. Seven verses later, his name was going to change to Paul. It is not uncommon that when God does a remarkable work of transforming a person, a new name emerges. Think Abram to Abraham (Father of a Multitude), Sarai to Sarah (A Princess), Jacob to Israel (Struggled with God), Gideon to Jerub-Baal (Slayer/fighter of Baal), Cephas to Peter (Rock), etc. Paul was a remarkable man whose influence in the early church and in the writing of the New Testament cannot be overstated.

This was a tremendously eclectic group, but what divided them racially, economically, and culturally was meaningless when brought into the light of what united them spiritually and ministerially. They each had a solid and growing relationship with Jesus Christ through faith in him and had been called into the leadership of this church by God's Holy Spirit. It was in that unity that we find them together in Acts 13.

And what were they doing? What was their mindset when God chose to break into their normal lives and tell them to commission 40% of the top leadership of their team to intentional ministry to bring the love of God and the message of Jesus to unreached people?

*"While they were worshiping the Lord and fasting, the Holy Spirit said, "Set apart for me, Barnabas and Saul for the work to which I have called them." (Acts 13:2)*

These men were about to embark on the first deliberate spreading of the Good News to the masses of unreached people in the then-known world. The work to which God called them, was the third sequel in the movie trilogy: "Acts 1:8 - Phase III: To the Ends of the Earth."

But notice this detail, because it is very, very instructive. The moment at which their spirits were most sensitive to the call of God's Spirit to commission them to Phase III of his plans to reach the unreached was when they were worshiping!

It should not surprise us that those who are engaged in true worship are most sensitive to the need for true mission. Why?

Because of the nature of worship. Our word worship comes, unsurprisingly, from the old word worth-ship. Worship is ascribing to the Lord his true worth. Worship is a passion to assure that in my words, in my life, in my community, and in my world, God is seen with his true worth and the glory he has.

*"Ascribe to the LORD, families of nations, ascribe to the LORD, glory and strength. Ascribe to the LORD, the glory due his name; bring an offering and come into his courts. Worship the LORD in the splendor of his holiness; tremble before him all the earth. Say among the nations, the LORD reigns." (Psalm 96:7-10)*

Worship is ascribing to the LORD (Yahweh, the true God), the glory that is due him because of who he is and what he has done. It is declaring his worth.

How does this fit together with reaching the unconvinced on the other side of my street and the unreached on the other side of my world? Here's how: If I truly love God; if I am truly worshiping God; if I am truly passionate that He is seen with the glory he deserves, then I cannot remain unmoved by the fact that blinded or beguiled people around the world are attempting to rob God of his glory. They are misrepresenting His worth, saying untrue things about Him, His character, and His actions, living in ignorance and fear of Him when they could be living in His knowledge and love. They are worshiping and serving created things rather than the true God as their creator. That vexes the hearts of those who are passionate about God's glory.

Let me see if I can illustrate. I love my wife. I want her to be seen as the remarkable, beautiful, gracious, loving, committed, and sacrificial woman she is. If I knew that people were speaking lies about her then I would be moved to set the record straight! And I would not wait to be asked.

Let me try to ask this question with as much grace as possible directed at myself as well. And please forgive me if I don't.

Married men and women, if you permit others to insult your spouse, if you have no passion to guard their reputation, if you can let go unchallenged falsehoods and sleights directed at your partner, then are you loving them well? Are you concerned that their true worth be shown and known?

Christians, if you can permit others, in your presence or on the other side of the world, to insult, misrepresent, and mischaracterize. God, and yet have no passion to set the record straight and tell them of his true glorious worth, might you need to examine whether your "worship" is really God-centered worth-ship or just self-centered emotion or dead-cold tradition?

I am afraid that some of what passes as worship today is more about how I feel than about how God is seen.

True worship cannot be divorced from a true passion for the unreached to know Christ and glorify him. Concern for the Glory of God compels us to reach the unreached.

# Chapter - 7
# THE PRIVILEGE OF SETTING CAPTIVES FREE

"How'd that make you feel; giving a child his freedom?"

"It felt good!"

"You've been at this for 12 years. Why are you doing it?"

"Because God's children are not for sale."

With those simple statements in the 2023 film Sound of Freedom, the main character Tim Ballard gives the reason he left a secure job with the US government and launched out on a dangerous, costly, and risky mission to rescue children who have been sold and trafficked into slavery.

There are few earthly horrors that can compare with the unspeakable evil practice of enslaving children for the domestic servitude or sexual pleasure of adults. Correspondingly, there must be few earthly privileges like being the person that God uses to free a captive child from such bondage.

How much deeper is the privilege of being used by God to set captives free from the horrors of spiritual slavery that, if uninterrupted, will lead to the eternal horrors mentioned in chapter 4 of this book?

As the end of his life drew near, the Apostle Paul could feel it in his bones and in his spirit. He sat in a Roman prison, and the longing for heaven seemed to grow daily.

Seven years earlier, he had called himself *"an old man"* *(Philemon 9)*. Shortly after that, while in another prison, he had confessed that *"I eagerly expect, and hope that I will in no way be ashamed, but will have sufficient courage that now, as always, Christ will be exalted in my body, whether by life or by death. For to me, to live is Christ, and to die is gain... I am torn between the two. I desire to depart and be with Christ, which is better by far..." (Philippians 2:20-23)*

Now, as he sat confined, he penned a letter (or more likely dictated it) to his young son in the faith, Timothy. This letter was one of his last known writings, and he acknowledges, *"For I am already being poured out as a drink offering, and the time has come for my departure. I have fought the good fight, I have finished the race, I have kept the faith. Now there is in store for me a crown..." (II Timothy 4:6-8a)*

As he considers his departure from this earth, he recalls the departure of so many from him, and from true faith in Christ. *"You know that everyone in the province of Asia has deserted me, even Phygelus and Hermogenes." (II Timothy 1:15)* *"Demas, because he loved the world, has deserted me..." (II Timothy 4:10)* *"Alexander the metalworker did me a great deal of harm. The Lord will repay him for what he has done. You too should be on your guard against him, because he strongly opposed our message. At my first defense, no one came to my support, but everyone deserted me." (II Timothy 4:16)*

Paul had felt the sting of personal and doctrinal betrayal. He knew that the drumbeat of opposition did not stop with his imprisonment and would not stop with his death.

To Timothy, whom he had addressed as his *"dear son" (II Timothy 1:2)* and his *"true son in the faith" (I Timothy 1:2)*,

Paul gives heartfelt, and probably heartbroken, instructions on how to minister in the midst of such opposition.

Paul knew, as you do, that there are always going to be those who will deny the message and defy the messenger of God. They will, sometimes even after claiming to believe, disagree with and dispute over the truth.

At the time I am writing this book, there is a movement in the United States Christendom of people "deconstructing" their faith. After doing so for themselves, rather than building others up, some seem intent on breaking down the faith of others. With sadness, I confess that some percentage of the blame for this falls, it seems to me, at the feet of those of us who have been leaders of churches that have offered an incomplete vision of a life where transformation is to be expected when living a life of faith in Christ.

We discovered in Chapter 1, that Christ's Great Commission is to lead people to faith in him, and to maturity in that faith. May the Lord show us any culpability, any area that needs adjustment, and may we repent quickly.

My point in this chapter is not to point fingers at our shortcomings. (That would take another book or several). It is just to acknowledge that there is ever-growing and ever-louder opposition to God's message of salvation and sanctification. Paul had mentioned this to Timothy in II Timothy 3:14 where he says, *"evil men and imposters will go from bad to worse, deceiving and being deceived."*

My point in this chapter is to emphasize what Paul said about how to respond to opposition, or more particularly to opposers. Many books have been written about what to respond, but let's ask how to respond. What should our mindset, our attitude, and our demeanor be, when facing opposition? And what beliefs make possible that demeanor?

*"And the Lord's servant must not be quarrelsome; instead, he must be kind to everyone, able to teach, not resentful. Those who oppose him must be gently instructed..." (II Timothy 2:24-25a)*

Timothy was the Lord's servant. So are you, Ambassador. So am I.

Look at the description of our prescribed demeanor toward opponents. Not quarrelsome, kind to everyone, not resentful, gentle.

Why? Why should I not be quarrelsome? Why should I not be bombastic and bellicose? Why should I be kind to people who oppose me?

Because there is a greater goal in mind. There is a higher value. There is a wider hope. We are not in a discussion just to win an argument.

What do we want to accomplish? *"In the hope that God will grant them repentance, leading them to a knowledge of the truth, and that they will come to their senses and escape from the trap of the devil, who has taken them captive to do his will."* *(II Timothy 2:24-26)*

The hope is that a person would repent. Repentance is a change of mind, it's a change of thoughts, it's a change of view, and it's a change of direction. It's deciding that what I was believing, and what I was following is not going to get me where I am aiming to go, so I'm going to change my mind and I'm going to go in a different direction.

As it relates to the initial entry into God's family, what the Bible calls being "born again" or "saved," most people have put their hope in something to get them to Heaven (and to give them purpose in life). The sad reality is that the vast majority of our world's population sincerely trusts in something that is sincerely untrustworthy.

In June of 2023, five men stepped into a small submarine called the Titan Submersible to take a journey deep into the North Atlantic Ocean to view the wreckage of the R.M.S. Titanic which sits on the ocean floor almost two and a half miles below the wave-swept surface. Each of them sincerely trusted the craft they entered. Each of them died 105 minutes later in a "catastrophic implosion" when the ocean pressure wrecked the Titan before ever reaching the wreckage of the Titanic. They sincerely trusted in something that was sincerely untrustworthy.

If a person is trusting something that is not worthy of their trust, then they need to change their mind and direction, or the consequences will be catastrophic. This is true in earthly things and is infinitely truer in spiritual things.

In the case of the people Paul mentions in II Timothy, he says he wants them to come to repentance. Why? What happens when a person comes to repentance? Paul tells us several things. First, it will lead them to a knowledge of the truth. Throughout this letter, Paul repeatedly references the truth which was known and accepted by Timothy but rejected and opposed by others. That truth, reflected in the Holy Scriptures, is what led Timothy to be *"wise for salvation which is through faith in Christ Jesus." (II Timothy 3:15)*

What is the hope for someone who knows the truth? That they will come to their senses.

The prodigal son whom we met in Chapter 5 of this book realized that his life was heading in the wrong direction and he turned around. *"When he came to his senses, he said, 'How many of my father's hired men have food to spare, and here I am starving to death! I will set out and go back to my father…'"* *(Luke 15:17)*

And I've taken you this far into the II Timothy 2 passage to get to the last phrase: *"and escape the trap of the devil, who is taking them captive to do his will."* *(II Timothy 2:26)*

The word used here for trap refers to an animal trap. A device that is hidden in order to ensnare prey and capture them for the trapper's own pleasure and purpose. The devil, the adversary of God, is consistently trying to snare people and keep them from understanding the truth, to keep them from coming to their senses, to keep them from escaping his trap.

In every corner of the world, the devil has beguiled and deceived people into believing a lie and now they are prisoners of the devil's deceptions and captive to do his will.

Understanding this concept is critical to developing a God-like heart of unending compassion towards those who are far from God; for those who are opposing God's truth, God's plan, and God's people.

Understanding this concept is what allowed Jesus, at the very moment that the opposers were crucifying him to petition, *"Father forgive them, they don't know what they are doing." (Luke 23:34)* With kindness and gentleness, he pleads for extended forgiveness because his opponents are in a trap, they don't understand, and they haven't come to their senses. They're captivated by the devil and his deception. It's what led Stephen to be able to say, in the midst of being stoned to death, *"Lord, do not hold this sin against them." (Acts 7:60)*

Jesus said of the Devil that *"When he lies, he speaks his native language, for he is a liar and the father of lies." (John 8:44)*

When's the devil lying? Whenever his lips are moving. The devil is a liar and the father of lies and his lies have convinced people to follow a path that will ultimately lead to their own destruction. He has trapped people in philosophies and religions and lifestyles that have imprisoned them.

The enemies of God's truth and of God's grace are not simply the opposers, they're the dupes of the real opposer. They're the captives, they're trapped by the devil into believing a lie and living it out. And there are billions of people all around the world in that lamentable situation.

This truth came to me in a life-changing moment in 1986. Let me give you some context. My father was a pilot in the United States Air Force. He was the boss of the plane. He rose to the rank of Lt. Colonel. Just before he retired, he was the Deputy Base Commander of an Air Force Base. Outside of the General, he was the boss of the base. He ran our family in the same way: he was the boss of the family. Dad had many good qualities, or he would not have succeeded like he did. But he was harsh, he was demanding, and he was distant. He was a hard-living man. He was an alcoholic and a serial adulterer.

When as a teen I came to faith in Christ, my father, after an initial period of nonchalance, opposed my faith and my lifestyle.

Jesus had changed my life and I wanted to tell others about Him. When I decided to leave the college engineering track to go to a Bible College and study the Bible, he told me that I was wasting my life.

My father did not want me to follow Jesus in a way that changed my life. He tried to reason with me and that did not work. He tried to argue with me and that did not work. He tried to threaten me and that did not work. So, he did with me what an officer does when he has an insubordinate subordinate. He took me to the General.

We sat by the General's pool in the heat of a Florida morning, and I shared with him how Jesus had changed my life and that all I really wanted to do was to learn how to share Him with others who had not heard of him. The General listened for about a half hour. I think my dad listened with the expectation that I would be convinced by his logic or compelled by his authority.

After I had my say, the General had his. He said, "This is what we'll do." (I thought to myself, "I don't think that WE are going to do anything"… but you don't say that to the General). He continued, "We'll send you to the Air Force Academy. You are an honor student and an athlete and a patriot and so that will be no problem. You can even be a chaplain if you want to." (I knew that was not something that he could offer… but you don't say that to the General).

Finally, he said something that I hope I never forget. He leaned toward me and seriously, almost as an order, said, "Son, be religious if you want to, but don't let it ruin your life." At the time I realized that, in flight lingo, we were listening to completely different control towers.

When I took a stand and made the decision to drop my engineering major and go to Bible College, my father took his stand. He told me that when I walked out the door, the door was going to shut and remain that way. And he was a man of his word in that area. It led to a very difficult and strained relationship for years, in both directions.

He felt disrespected and I felt disowned.

After my dad retired from the military, he went from being a Deputy Base Commander in Florida to just another retiree in Florida, and he couldn't handle it. What was previously a part-time job of being a functioning alcoholic became his full-time passion. He drank himself into a condition where he did brain damage to himself and was in a car accident. And I got a call from the court system that said, "Your father is now being declared legally incompetent, and you need to be his guardian." Those were challenging days.

In the same month that we had our first son and launched a new church, we brought my dad to live with us in our one-bedroom apartment. So, the stress-o-meter was pretty much hitting the wall.

A couple of days later in the middle of the night, I heard a sickening loud thump in the bathroom of our small apartment. I raced in and found my father lying on the floor, bloodied because he had struck his head, and was going into a seizure.

As Nancy called the paramedics, I held my dad as he convulsed so that he wouldn't do any further damage to himself. When he finally stopped, I sat on the floor of our minuscule bathroom with the limp body of my father draped across my lap. The man was emaciated physically, spiritually, emotionally, and intellectually;

reduced from a once-strong warrior who could command troops, to a limp body.

And at that moment, in that very moment, I realized as I looked down at my father, that God had changed my heart toward my dad. I no longer saw him as just a victimizer, I saw him as a victim.

He was a man who had been snared by the devil; trapped into believing a lie about life and eternity. A man who had lived in the consistent belief of that lie which had rendered him captive. A man who had spent his one and only life on a forgery that promised blessings but delivered bondage.

On the bathroom floor, I realized that God had done a work in my heart, replacing the anger that I had felt toward my father with intense compassion and a depth of sadness that probably cannot be expressed. This man was a victim! God had changed my heart by changing my view.

And in a real way, that's what I'm calling us to today. I want God to change our hearts by changing our view of people who are without Christ. People who have never had the chance to understand who he is, who have never made the choice to accept him, or maybe have made the choice to reject him. Because they are victims. In a world that follows lies, there are billions of individual people who are captives of the Liar.

While speaking about Jesus and his death on our behalf, Hebrews 2:14b-15 explains, *"...so that by his death he might destroy him that has the power of death - that is, the devil, and free those who all their lives were held in slavery by the fear of death."*

Billions of people in our world are enslaved by Satan in a prison of fear of death because no one has offered them the key to freedom that you and I as believers in Christ have in our possession.

Why do people fear death?

Let's briefly look at I Corinthians 15. It is the central Biblical text if you want to look at the meaning of the resurrection. The Apostle Paul writes about that future moment...

*"When the perishable has been clothed with the imperishable, and the mortal with immortality, then the saying that is written will come true: 'Death has been swallowed up in victory. Where, O death, is your victory? Where, O death, is your sting? The sting of death is sin, and the power of sin is the law. But thanks be to God! He gives us the victory through our Lord Jesus Christ."*
*(I Corinthians 15:54-57)*

Paul quotes from the Old Testament. It's like he's trash-talking death. He says, "Death, is that all you got? Come on, bring it on! You got no sting! You sting like a butterfly!" How can he do that? Verse 56 explains that *"The sting of death is sin, and the power of sin is the law."*

Why is death so fearful to people? Why is it stinging? Because we know that there is sin. People fear death because of an uncertain future.

I don't fear that of which I am certain. I don't fear going through the doorway of my house because I know what's on the other side and it's not bad. But people fear death because they don't know what's on the other side of the threshold. It's uncertain to them.

People fear an uncertain future because of a certain coming judgment. They intuitively know that there is a judgment coming. Read Romans chapters 1-3. Deep in their psyche, informed by their conscience, people know that there is something else out there, someone out there to whom they are accountable. They know that they will ultimately have to answer for their thoughts and deeds, their actions and inactions and they fear that they are not ready.

People are fearful of judgment because they are aware of sin. They know that they haven't lived up to the standard that even they set for themselves, never mind the one that God sets for us. And therefore, there's fear of death.

I see this all over the world.

And people try by any means possible to escape their slavery to the fear of death. They try denial: "Oh it's not real, it's not there, it's not going to happen." They try prolonging life unnaturally: "I'll be alive forever." They try religion. And we could tell story after story after story of people who simply substitute religion for trying to live up to the standard and trying to figure out how they can escape slavery to the fear of death.

But there is good news. There's a key to the prison. And that's the exciting message that we have to offer. No one needs to live in fear of death! The key to freedom is laid out in the first verses of that chapter.

*"Now, brothers and sisters, I want to remind you of the gospel [the good news] I preached to you, which you received and on which you have taken your stand. By this good news, you are saved... For what I received I passed on to you as of first importance: that Christ died for our sins according to the*

*Scriptures, that he was buried, that he was raised on the third day according to Scriptures…" (I Corinthians 15:1-4)*

Christ died for our sins. Therefore, if we've accepted his free gift of eternal life and salvation, our sins are forgiven and no longer have a death grip on us. We've been reconciled to God. We've been forgiven for all our sins. He has paid the punishment. There's no fear. There's no terror in that.

The key that unlocks the prison and frees people from captivity to fear and to the devil, is the sweet gospel of Jesus Christ. Sins are forgiven in Christ, therefore there is no fear of judgment for those sins. Where there is no fear of judgment there is no fear of death. Since there is no fear of death, I can live in abandoned surrender and in freedom. And while living in freedom I have the unspeakable privilege and the inescapable responsibility of making sure that the key to freedom that I have in my hand is offered to captives worldwide.

And if I truly understand my emancipation, how could I not desire that other people have the key that will free them? How can I not be concerned? How can I withhold the key that would open their locks and free these prisoners?

This is the seventh reason why I should do my part to reach unreached people: The privilege of being the one God uses to set captives free.

But let's end by asking and answering another short question: If that is the "Why" answer, what is the "When" answer? My answer is "Now!"

Because first, I believe that the Spirit of God is moving today. I think there are people who are reading this book and realize that "I've stepped over the line of faith, I want to obey Christ's command, I want to glorify him, I want others to be set free." If the Spirit of the Lord is speaking today don't harden your heart. Do something. Do *something*.

In the second section of this book, I will tell you how God led some of us to respond to these challenges and I will invite you to join us. I'll give you permission to skip over the next few chapters in order to respond quickly if the Lord is moving. (You can read the rest later).

Second, because there is no guarantee of tomorrow. Over 150,000 people who are alive today will not be alive tomorrow. Over the course of the next week, 1,200,000 people who started today on Earth with us, will not be on Earth any longer. For them, there is no tomorrow. If they die while still being held captive to Satan's trap of unbelief or believing a lie, then their eternal prison will be worse than their current prison.

There are billions of people in Satan's captivity, and I hold the key to setting captives free! It is the Good News of Jesus. That's the exciting part; that we, you and I, can be used by God to set captives free.

The key that was used to unlock the prison and allow you and me to step out into the freedom of a relationship with God with the certainty of Heaven forever rests in our hands. And it is a privilege to use it to set captives free.

# Chapter - 8
# THE RESPONSIBILITY OF THE WATCHMAN

Someone has said that the Bible comforts the afflicted and afflicts the comfortable. I take that to mean that at times God uses the Scripture to prick the hearts and consciences of people who are comfortable in their lives and need to be prodded toward beliefs or actions that more closely align with God's will for them.

He does that through scriptural precepts (direct statements of what we should believe and how we should behave), scriptural principles (truths that, if applied to life, will mold the way we believe and behave), and scriptural practices (the example/model of godly people which God uses to influence the way we believe and behave).

In multiple congregations in which my family has fellowshipped in the past, I have had the deep privilege and even deeper responsibility of being recognized as an Elder. When considering the role of an Elder and whether I could bear this heavy responsibility, I have often returned to Acts chapter 20 and the Apostle Paul's admonition to the Elders in the church at Ephesus.

For the purposes of this chapter, I will not unpack the entirety of Paul's heart-rending and humble challenge to these men as they were to *"keep watch over yourselves and all the flock of which the Holy Spirit has made you overseers." (Acts 20:28)* But one declaration Paul makes about himself and his ministry challenges me to the core of my ministry calling as both an Elder and as a minister of the Good News. And I believe it has application to me as a Christian regardless of my vocation.

*Therefore, I declare to you today that I am innocent of the blood of all men. For I have not hesitated to proclaim to you the whole will of God. (Acts 20:26-27)*

Innocent of the blood of another person? What does that mean? Paul clearly expresses that his innocence (or guilt) hinges on whether he has proclaimed to his hearers what God has given him, the revelation of the will of God.

Whoa. That is a heavy concept. Is there, somehow, a guilt that accrues to the account of a person who, having been given the responsibility of warning those who are in danger, hesitates to do so?

In writing about guilt and innocence as it relates to a ministry assignment, it seems obvious to me that Paul's mind, which was steeped in Old Testament precepts, principles, and practices, transports effortlessly to Ezekiel 3.

*At the end of seven days, the word of the LORD came to me: "Son of man, I have made you a watchman for the people of Israel; so hear the word I speak and give them warning from me. When I say to a wicked person, 'You will surely die,' and you do not warn them or speak out to dissuade them from their evil ways in order to save their life, that wicked person will die for their sin, and I will hold you accountable for their blood. But if you do warn the wicked person and they do not turn from their wickedness or from their evil ways, they will die for their sin; but you will have saved yourself." (Ezekiel 3:16-19)*

71

# DANGER AND DUTY

The only reason to appoint a watchman is that there is a danger that they need to recognize and relay. Where there is no peril, there need be no probing.

Dotting the mid-Atlantic seaboard of the USA, just south of where I live, are 11 cylindrical concrete towers. Each rise between 50 and 64 feet above the coastal marshes and sandy beaches. Each has an observation deck near the top which allows for an unrestricted view of up to 20 miles of the Atlantic coastline and sea routes.

The towers were built between 1939 and 1942 at a cost of less than $18,000 each. These towers were built because of a clear and eminent danger: Nazi ships. During World War II, German ships, both surface and submarine, made their way to the area, intent on attacking the US eastern seaboard's vital shipping lanes. For periods of the war, they sank one US ship per week.

The danger was real and deadly.

It was in response to this danger that the towers were erected, and soldiers enlisted to man them. Each tower had a team of men who were given the sacred duty of being watchmen. The watchman was to scan the area of their assignment and remain awake, alert, and aware, and to sound alarm at danger to his charges.

When Watchmen identified the impending attack, they would sound a warning and radio the coordinates of the enemy ship to one of several artillery batteries. Using the coordinates from multiple towers, the large defensive guns within concealed coastal forts would ready themselves by triangulating the position of the adversarial crafts. When commanded, they would fire 2700-pound shells from 12-inch and 16-inch barrels. This massive artillery could fire up to 25 miles at the enemy.

Nobody knows how many lives were saved because these watchmen fulfilled their duties.

## DECISION AND DISCHARGE

The discharge of the duty required a decision.

Each soldier had a choice to make. Fulfilling their calling was not easy and not free of risk. Each day they would climb rope ladders, five stories inside the cylindrical watch towers to gain access to the observation perch. The enemy, for obvious reasons, would silence them if they could, through violence, or fear, discouragement, or boredom.

But a faithful soldier would dismiss the hardship and hazard and fulfill the requirements of the role. What were the requirements of a watchman?

### Stay Awake

The Hebrew word used in Ezekiel 3 for a watchman is "tsaphah" which conveys the idea of being fully aware of a situation in order to gain some advantage or keep from being surprised by an enemy. More than any word, it describes the special characteristic of Ezekiel's work, for he was to watch personally over individual souls.

C.H. Spurgeon comments that one of the devices of Satan is that he "seeks to lull God's prophets into slumber, for he knows that dumb dogs that are given to sleep will never do any very great injury to his cause. The wakeful watchmen, he always fears, for he cannot take the city by surprise; but if he can cast God's watchman into slumber, then he is well content, and thinks it almost as well to have a Christian asleep as to have him dead: he would certainly sooner see him in hell, but next to that, he is most glad to see him rocked in the cradle of presumption, fast asleep."

It matters not whether a watchman sleeps due to their own negligent use of their time or lack of discipline prior to commencing their watch or whether on their watch they are lulled to sleep by boredom or whether they are knocked on the head by an enemy or whether they are hypnotized by some distraction. The result is the same. The enemy is free to attack undisturbed, and the watchman fails his duty.

## Stand Alert

Years ago, I was told to "Be alert because the world needs more lerts!" I thought it was silly and childish and yet funny then, and still do. Maybe that tells you more about me than you want to know.

Remaining awake is of no value if the watchman is not alert. They do not discharge their duty if they are awake but playing a game of cards or amusing themselves into distractedness.

By the way, did you know that the word amuse comes from the prefix "a" which negates what comes after, and the word "muse," which means to think, meditate, or ponder? So, amusement is the act of being in a state of "no-think." That is fine and even required sometimes but not while on watch duty.

There is no shortage of biblical admonition to remain alert.

But all the vigilance to recognize duty and danger will not fulfill the watchman's mission, unless, having seen the danger, he sounds the alarm.

## Sound Alarm

God told Ezekiel to speak. *"Hear the word I speak and give them warning from me." (Ezekiel 3:17)*. Early in the same chapter, God told Ezekiel, *"Son of Man, listen carefully and take to heart all the words I speak to you. Go now to your countrymen in exile and speak to them. Say to them, 'This is what the sovereign LORD says,' whether they listen, or fail to listen." (Ezekiel 3:10-11)*

Ezekiel's job was to grasp God's word and then give God's message. Sounds like it is pretty much the same for us. Notice that Ezekiel was not responsible for the response. God even told him, *"But the house of Israel is not willing to listen to you, because they are not willing to listen to me..." (Ezekiel 3:7)*

To discharge his duty, the watchmen must remain at his post. I think C.H Spurgeon gives a clear picture:

> When a sentinel is set upon the watch, he must not come off without the commander's leave, and till he is discharged by authority. God hath set us in a watch, and we must not leave our ground till we have done all that is enjoined upon us and receive a fair discharge. The instance of the sentinel in Pompeii, whose skeleton was found erect at the city gate, when all but he had fled, need not be repeated in words; but it should be copied by each one of us in his life. If the earth should reel, it is ours to keep our place. If set to preach the Gospel, let us maintain the truth, though philosophy should thin the number of our comrades till we remain alone. Imagine what the universe would be if the stars forsook their marches, and the sun forbore to shine; yet this would only be among inanimate objects an

75

imitation of the conduct of men who quit their posts, and leave their work undone. This is the spirit out of which fiends are made: first neglect, then omission, then treachery and rebellion. A sentinel must not leave his post even to gather pearls or diamonds; nor must we forsake our duty in order to acquire the highest honors. It matters nothing how well we have done other things if we neglect the thing. God bids us to do **this**, and if we fail it will be no excuse to be able to say we have done **that**. If the watcher forsakes his post, it will not avail that he climbed a mountain or swam a river: he was not where he was ordered to be.

## DESTRUCTION AND DELIVERANCE

What difference does it make if the watchman does his job? All the difference in the world and in eternity.

Peter announces that God is *"not wanting anyone to perish, but everyone to come to repentance." (II Peter 3:9)*

As we have seen throughout this book, salvation happens when people are warned of the danger and wooed by the Spirit into a saving faith in Jesus Christ. The result is an escape from the reality of hell, deliverance from the penalty of our sins, and welcome into the forever family of God.

This is the importance of the watchman's duty.

Here, though, we must be reminded that, even if the watchman flawlessly performs his assignment, the results are in the hand of another. *"Unless the Lord guards, a city, the watchmen stays awake in vain." (Psalm 127:1)*

So, we watch and warn, and we pray that the work of the Holy Spirit means that our proclamation of the Good News is not in vain but leads to deliverance.

## DETERMINATION AND DECREE

Here, for me, is the great challenge of Ezekiel's commission and ours.

Throughout the sweep and scope of scripture, God's revelation is clear concerning the means of my salvation and the continuity of it. So, what does it mean that the silent watchmen will be accountable for the blood of the unwarned? What does it mean that a church Elder will *"give an account"* for their wakeful watch over the souls of the congregation (Hebrews 13:17)? What does it mean that Paul was innocent of the blood of others because he shared, publicly, and from house to house, as he *"declared to both Jews and Greeks, that they must turn to God in repentance, and have faith in our Lord Jesus Christ"* as he says in Acts 20:20-21?

First, it cannot mean that Ezekiel or any other watchmen will lose their eternal salvation because of a lapse in fulfillment of their duty.

It cannot mean that Ezekiel or any other watchmen will receive the punishment of the person who perishes. The person who parishes has already received that punishment.

It seems clear that the consequence of the unfaithfulness of a watchman includes divine chastening and loss of eternal rewards. Read I Corinthians chapters 3 and 4 where Paul explains that God will examine our ministry and determine its worth and declares:

*By the grace God has given me, I laid a foundation as a wise builder, and someone else is building on it. But each one should build with care. For no one can lay any foundation other than the one already laid, which is Jesus Christ. If anyone builds on this foundation using gold, silver, costly stones, wood, hay or straw, their work will be shown for what it is, because the Day will bring it to light. It will be revealed with fire, and the fire will test the quality of each person's work. If what has been built survives, the builder will receive a reward. If it is burned up, the builder will suffer loss but yet will be saved - even though only as one escaping through the flames. (I Cor. 3:10-15)*

Larry Richards, in *The 365-day Devotional Commentary*, applies this truth to believers pointing out: "Today it's helpful if we think of each Christian's 'job description' in the same way [as Ezekiel's]. It takes no special qualification to serve our neighbors as a watchman. No seminary degree is required. Not even mastery of Scripture, or great spiritual depth. All that's called for is awareness that friends without Christ are in terrible peril - and a voice to lift to give them warning. We can't guarantee that any individual will respond. But if we remain silent, we carry some responsibility for that other's fate. A word of warning to another clears us of guilt and may lead him or her to eternal life."

We who, by faith, know Jesus Christ as our savior, and are in Christ; as believers, as ambassadors, as watchmen, have a responsibility to be God's mouthpiece to warn people in danger and offer them the safety of salvation.

The watchman was assigned to warn those within the city walls. They had a specific charge, given to them regarding for whom they were to watch out, and to whom they were to sound the alarm. Considering that, the question arises: Who is within the walls of my influence and responsibility? For whom has God made me a watchman?

After reading the Scriptures and spending much of my life imperfectly attempting to follow the precepts of God's Word, the principles of God's revelation, the practices of God's people, and the promptings of God's Spirit, I am compelled to believe that I am, and each Christian is, responsible as a watchman over as many people as God gives us the strength to warn. Let's commit ourselves to fulfilling our sacred responsibility and bring the loud and clarion-clear message of warning and message of salvation to as many people as God will give us the opportunity.

# Chapter - 9
# THE OBLIGATION TO THE UNREACHED

We are living in a sinful, fallen, and broken world! Our world, our country, our communities, our families and so many individual lives are in major crisis, and in many ways, imploding before our eyes. There are many conflicting voices that are being raised about what is wrong.

From a biblical perspective, what is the primary problem in all these areas? The primary problem in our world is not a political problem. The primary problem in our world is not a racial problem. The primary problem in our world is not a social problem. The primary problem in our world is not a financial or economic problem. The primary problem in our world is not an educational problem.

There are political, racial, social, financial, and educational problems in every country around this broken world, but these problems are just "symptoms." The root cause of our problems is the rejection of God, the suppression of biblical truth, and the failure of the church of Jesus Christ to faithfully proclaim the love-filled and grace-filled gospel of Jesus Christ to our world.

The only hope for the future of our world, and each individual in it, is a revival in the church of Jesus Christ which causes a revolutionary commitment to offering the Gospel, the solitary solution to the paramount problem of humanity. We can, and should, help heal the wounds of hearts and societies, but we must not fall into the trap of believing that temporal solutions will solve eternal problems.

The gospel of Jesus Christ alone is the power of God unto salvation. The gospel of Jesus Christ alone has the power to transform hearts, lives, communities, cultures, and ultimately our world.

The purpose of this book is to invite the Spirit of God to ignite a passion in our lives so that we understand, flourish in, and share the Good News of Jesus Christ with those who have not heard it plainly in a way to which they can respond in faith and begin a transformational relationship with him.

Because He is our only hope, I believe we owe it to the unreached and the unconvinced to make known by a life they can witness and a language they can understand that the Gospel of Jesus is *"the power of God for the salvation of everyone who believes." (Romans 1:16)*

My friend, Mark Crocco, shares that there are three passionate attitudes that will motivate us to reach out to others in our broken world. They are unearthed in Romans 1:14-17 which contains the expression of Paul's passion for the gospel and for people.

*I am obligated both to the Greeks and to the Barbarians; both to the wise and to the unwise. That is why I am eager to preach the gospel also to you that are at Rome. For I am not ashamed of the gospel of Christ: because it is the power of God unto salvation to everyone who believes; first for the Jew, then for the Gentile. For in the gospel a righteousness from God is revealed, a righteousness that is by faith from first to last, just as it is written, "The righteous shall live by faith." (Romans 1:14-17)*

81

Note the three "**I am**" statements Paul makes. In verse 14 he says, "**I am** under obligation." In verse 15 he says, "**I am** eager to preach the gospel." In verse 16 he says, "**I am** not ashamed of the gospel." Let's unpack each of those.

## I AM UNDER OBLIGATION

When our purpose in life is rooted in the gospel we will reach out to our broken world with a spirit of indebtedness. Paul unashamedly admits that he is currently, and also in an ongoing state, of debt. The same man who said, *"Owe no man anything, but to love one another: for he that loves another hath fulfilled the law" (Romans 13:8)*, tells us that he is living in a continual state where he owes people something.

In Walt Disney's 1937 classic animated film *Snow White and the Seven Dwarfs*, the collection of heartwarming little characters with amusingly big hats leave Snow White alone at home while they head off to the mines to labor. As they depart, they sing, "Heigh-ho, Heigh-ho, it's off to work I go." Some financially strapped humorist quipped, "I owe, I owe. So, it's off to work, I go." I'd like to steal that ditty to illustrate Paul's attitude toward his obligation to share the Good News. Sing along: "I owe, I owe. So, off to share I go!"

First, let's look at what he means by being under obligation. And then let's see to whom he is under obligation.

I wish that I could be brilliant and nuanced in bringing out some deep hidden meaning in this passage. But the simple truth is that the truth is simple. The word he uses for debt or to owe (*"opheílô"*) just means to owe, be indebted, to be obliged to rectify a debt. One word study says it refers to being morally obligated (or legally required) to meet an obligation, i.e., to pay off a legitimate debt.

As I said, the simple truth is that the truth is simple.

Paul says that he recognizes his moral, spiritual, and interpersonal indebtedness to others who have never heard or responded to the gospel. The gospel belongs to God, and He has entrusted it to Paul and all Christians through the ages... and to me. Elsewhere Paul proclaims that *"we speak as men approved by God to be entrusted with the gospel" (I Thessalonians 2:4).* Those who have been entrusted with something that belongs to another have an obligation to use that thing in fulfillment of that trust. The Bible refers to that as stewardship and *"it is required that those who have been given a trust must prove faithful."* *(I Corinthians 4:2)*

God has entrusted the gospel to humans to personalize it and to publicize it. Paul recognizes his stewardship debt to God often. But here, he indicates that there is a horizontal debt not just a vertical debt.

Paul states that he is obligated to both the Greeks and to the Barbarians, both to the wise and the foolish. He divides the entire world on the basis of culture (Greeks/barbarians) and education (the wise/foolish). The Roman church to whom Paul wrote was primarily Gentiles but he did not want them to get the idea that the Good News was for only people like them. Just like the Jewish-background believers had to learn that God's love and offer extended beyond them to the Gentiles, these Gentile-background believers had to learn that God's love extended beyond them to all the world.

To Paul's cultured and refined readers, the thought of joining a family with an uncultured and savage Barbarian was scandalous. To Paul's grad-school-educated hearers, the idea of sitting next to a hick from the sticks or a household servant whose advanced degree was from the school of hard knocks was mind-blowing. But Paul lays out his bottom line: I am indebted to "all" people. Not on the basis of education or financial status or race or ethnicity or sex or politics. The implication is that the fact that someone is a human who has yet to hear and understand the message that will save them creates an obligation to share it.

As we discussed in Chapter 1 on The Command of Christ, God has made it clear that He wants us to bring the Good News of His love and the offer of salvation and a growing relationship with Him to every person in every people group living under every social system in every inhabited place on every piece of dirt in the world.

The Pauline obligation, and my Christian obligation, are created by the presence of a deadly disease in my midst (sin) and a saving antidote in my hand (the message of the Good News). I owe the cure to the terminally ill and it is unthinkably immoral to withhold it.

As I write this, the world has recently emerged from a global pandemic of COVID-19. The virus and the medical and political prescriptions surrounding it have become maddeningly polarizing. But I believe there is one thing upon which all can agree: if I possessed the cure to this pandemic and I withheld it and let people die, I would be a monster.

## I AM EAGER

Paul had the answer to something more dangerous than COVID-19 and he had no intention of keeping the remedy to himself. In fact, when he considered sharing the lifesaving and eternity-saving message with the unreached, he describes his attitude as an outburst of passion. That is what the word translated *eager* means as he writes, *I am eager to preach the gospel to you that are at Rome also (verse 15).*

I am a sucker for unsuspecting reunion videos. You know the ones. There are an infinite number of plot details, but the story is always the same. A loved one (father, mother, child) is away for a long time (six months, a year, longer) on a noble cause (defending freedom, bringing justice, pursuing training) and is not expected to return until some later date. Secretly, cameras roll as the family of the loved one goes about normal life business only to be ambushed by the presence of the returnee. And what we witness is an outburst of passion. Shrieks of joy unleashed. Hugs that will not release. Children's bodies jump in euphoric anticipation that they cannot contain. If you can't get moist eyes at that, I worry about you.

That was Paul at the thought of saving lives with the message of the gospel.

Paul had the cure, and he was not begrudgingly offering it. He was not just willingly offering it. He was not just gladly offering it. He was filled with overwhelming excitement about offering it.

He was the dog who found a bone and waited at the door with his tail wagging uncontrollably to share it with his owner.

But sharing it was not going to be easy. He says that he was eager to share in Rome. Rome! A place of pervasive idolatry. But he was eager. A capital of rampant immorality. But he was eager. A seat of arrogant self-sufficiency. But he was eager. He would experience opposition, deprivation, mocking, and sacrifice. But he was eager.

This word "*eager*" was used in New Testament times of the "forward lean of a runner" waiting for the starter's gun to begin the race. It was used to describe a horse that was breathing heavily ready to charge into battle.

Have you ever noticed how eager we are to share life's good news? A couple gets engaged and they can't wait to share the good news. Before the young man's knee rises from the proposal ground the Instagram pictures are already posted.

A few months before I sat writing this sentence, I became a grandfather (for the first time) to a precious little girl. I know that many people have become grandparents before. I vowed that I was not going to be "that grandfather" who shares pictures of his grandkid with everyone he meets even when the audience was less than, well, eager. It became apparent, as I held my granddaughter, that those other grandparents did not have as remarkable a grandchild as I did.

I was, and am, enthralled by this remarkably adorable child who is so clearly advanced beyond other kids. And my vow of reserve went out the window as I scrolled through pictures to brag at every opportunity. I was eager to share the good news. I could not imagine depriving humanity of just a taste of the joy I experienced.

Can you see where I am going?

Why is it that we are so fervent to share about good-news life events and so hesitant to share about good-news eternal life events?

## I AM NOT ASHAMED

What is it about the gospel that makes Paul so eager to share it with others? The answer is found as he shares, *"For I am not ashamed of the gospel of Christ: because it is the power of God unto salvation to everyone who believes; first for the Jew, then for the Gentile." (Romans 1:16)*

I am not ashamed of the gospel. Let's be honest; there are some things that I am ashamed of in my 65-plus years of life. I have said, done, thought, and left undone some things that make me cringe even decades later. Paul had his own list of shameworthy things. But this is not about me, and it is not about Paul, and it is not about you. It is about the gospel.

Paul speaks here of a fitting shame for having associated myself with something or someone who brings disgrace. There is nothing disgraceful in the loving message of the gospel.

An alarming trend exists in the church of Jesus Christ in this "politically correct" world; the paralyzing desire not to offend. There is a reluctance to speak the truth in humility because we don't want to be seen as narrow or intolerant.

Over the years I have flown a lot of airline miles. Sometimes it is nice to engage in conversations. Often now, with the advent of noise-canceling headphones, I am more likely to greet those around me and retreat into some music, message, or podcast.

Many years ago, when conversing on planes was the norm, I found myself in the lower level of Hades (commonly referred to as the center seat). I am 6'4" tall and there are a lot of benefits to height. Air travel is not one of them.

I boarded and, knowing that it would be difficult to get my reading materials out of the overhead locker, I grabbed them from my backpack and tucked them into the seat-back pocket in front of me. I greeted the two pleasant ladies who arrived and took their seats on either side of me. They seemed to be having a conversation as they boarded which continued as we sat. They leaned forward and talked across me. As I listened, I discerned that they were discussing a hot-button political issue that had inescapable moral ramifications. This was a conversation that I had, if I am to be honest, little interest in joining. But the undesirable happened. One of the seatmates recognized that I was listening and asked, "So, what do you think?"

I (graciously I thought) shared some views about how the conclusions they agreed upon were actually downstream of some assumptions that I did not share. I said that I understood how they arrived at their shared consensus but that I was a Christian, I believed the Bible and my understanding of some fundamental realities brought me to a very different conclusion. I sat back believing that I had gently given them something to ponder. I was wrong.

I glanced to my side and could see a face contorting and lip quivering in anger. Finally, in a voice that could be heard all the way up in first class, one woman aggressively erupted, "How narrow can you be?"

I thought for a moment (and probably should have thought for several more), held up my thumb and pointer finger about 2 ½ inches apart, reached into the seat pocket in front of me, retrieved my Bible, slipped it between my fingers, and gently said, "About that narrow." It might not have been the best response, but it was a quiet flight.

We need not be ashamed of the gospel or of the Scripture. We need not be afraid of being viewed as offensive, intolerant, or narrow for graciously sharing the truth. The reality is, the message might be offensive, but the messenger should not be. Obviously, sometimes I fail at that.

Let's admit that sometimes the messengers have been off-putting (and that sometimes those messengers were us). But our loving obligation, our eagerness, and our unashamed belief in God's grace for all must not allow the resistance of the world, the flesh, or the devil to paralyze us into silence when we have the cure to a deadly disease. The ungraciousness of those who have shared the truth in the past should not mitigate the truthfulness of those who share grace today.

Paul looked beyond the possibility of unnerving some because he saw the possibility of unshackling some. He would risk defensiveness because he valued deliverance.

He said, *"I am not ashamed of the gospel of Christ."* Why? *"Because it is the power of God unto salvation to everyone who believes."*

The gospel holds the power to save. Jesus made it plain when he said that he is the way, the truth, and the life and that no one can come into a relationship with the Father except through Him (John 14:6).

Because the Gospel will save, I am not ashamed of it. Because I am not ashamed of it, I am eager to share it. Because God has given me the Gospel in trust, I owe it to the unreached to do my part to see that they have the opportunity to hear, understand, and respond to it.

# Chapter - 10
# THE REWARDS OF HEAVEN

Before you begin this chapter, note carefully that the word "rewards" in the title of this chapter is plural. That is not by accident. If I had left it singular (The Reward of Heaven), some might infer that I am implying that heaven is a reward for the work I have done on earth. It is not. Heaven is a free gift received as a blessing when I received Jesus Christ as my savior.

I say "Rewards of Heaven" because God, along with our entry into eternal dwellings with him, offers us a glimpse into some experiences in eternity. One of those things will be rewards given for work done on earth.

To those who are lost and estranged in separation from Him, God offers salvation as a free gift. To those who are saved and engaged in service for Him, God offers rewards as a result of what is done on earth.

I don't intend to offer an exhaustive study of rewards in the Scriptures. Many have done that earlier and better than I. What I want to offer is a simple suggestion: God offers rewards and commendation to create and sustain motivation in the lives of those who wish to follow him and advance His kingdom.

I'm not sure why he does that. Many have argued, with merit, that being in heaven with Christ should, and will, make any thoughts of rewards disappear in the joy of his presence. Some have argued that the mere consideration of finding heavenly rewards for fulfilling earthly responsibilities reeks of selfishness and has no place in our Christian experience or ministry. That is certainly worthy of discussion.

Maybe all of these reward debates would be moot if the vision of Revelation chapter 4 includes all believers.

Revelation 4 is the Apostle John's peek into heaven's throne room before the terrible judgment of the earth. Surrounding a central throne, are 24 other thrones, occupied by "24 elders."

As the narrative unfolds toward the crescendo of the opening of a seven-sealed scroll by the One sitting on the main throne, a worship service breaks out.

*"The 24 elders fall down before him who sits on the throne, and worship him who lives forever and ever. They lay their crowns before the throne, and say: 'You are worthy, our Lord and God, to receive glory and honor and power, for you created all things, and by your will they were created, and have their being.'"* *(Revelation 4:10-11)*

If in fact, as many conclude, the 24 elders represent the universal church of all true believers through all time; or if they even simply serve as a model for those who receive crowns and acknowledge that the rightful recipient of the reward should be the worthy Lord sitting on the throne who directed and empowered any effort that led to reward, then maybe rewards are okay. Could it be that, in the age to come, as it should be now, those who receive crowns or commendations will humbly worship our Lord and God, and proclaim his worthiness by deflecting any praise or glory toward Him? Could it be that the question, *"What do you have that you have not received?"* (asked in I Corinthians

4:7) will be answered loudly by heavenly crown-holders, "Nothing! Everything I have came from you, my Lord. I cannot keep this crown and I lay it at your feet as an act of worship. You are worthy!"

If a returned crown leads to Christ's renown, if a turned-back commendation leads to a turned-up adoration, then perhaps humbly doing what it takes to be on the "winners' podium" when crowns are given is worth it.

But I uncomfortably return to the nagging question: Why would God tell me about the crowns and commendations of my Master if it were not to spur me on to faithful and fruitful ministry?

So, awkwardly, I open my Bible to II Timothy 4, a portion of which we discussed earlier in chapter 7 of this book, and I read the Apostle Paul's pensive thoughts on his life as he approached his reward:

*"For I am already being poured out like a drink offering, and the time has come for my departure. I have fought the good fight, I have finished the race, I have kept the faith. Now, [Therefore], there is in store for me, the crown of righteousness, which the Lord, the righteous Judge, will award to me on that day - and not only to me, but also to all who have longed for his appearing."* (II Timothy 4:6-8)

As he contemplates the completion of his earthly race, Paul indicates that something remains to be experienced. The race is over, but the reward has not yet been given. And he seems to look forward to his crown.

Did he work hard? Did he voluntarily suffer to get the prize? He answers those questions in I Corinthians 9 when talking about his own desire to see people come to faith in Jesus.

The larger biblical context for the passage that I want us to consider at the end of I Corinthians 9 begins in I Corinthians 8. Apparently, answering one of the questions brought to him concerning Corinthian beliefs and practices, Paul discusses a Christian's willingness to sacrifice the exercise of their rights and liberties for a greater cause. In chapter 9, he relays that he had personally given up the right to eat certain foods, the right to marry, and the right to be supported as a Christian minister.

*"But we did not use this right. On the contrary, we put up with anything rather than hinder the gospel of Christ.... But I have not used any of those rights... Yet, when I preach the gospel, I cannot boast, for I am compelled to preach. Woe to me if I do not preach the gospel!" (I Corinthians 9:12, 15, 16)*

It is in that context that he answers the question of whether he will voluntarily subjugate his freedoms and rights to bring the Good News to those who are in bondage without Christ.

*Though I am free and belong to no one, I have made myself a slave to everyone, to win as many as possible. To the Jews I became like a Jew, to win the Jews. To those under the law I became like one under the law (though I myself am not under the law), so as to win those under the law. To those not having the law I became like one not having the law (though I am not free from God's law but am under Christ's law), so as to win those not having the law. To the weak I became weak, to win the weak. I have become all things to all people so that by all possible means I might save some. I do all this for the sake of the gospel, that I may share in its blessings. (I Corinthians 9:19-23)*

Why did he sacrifice so much? Why did he give up so much and take on so much? Why did he work so hard? Verse 19 tells us that it was to win as many as possible. Verse 20 tells us that it was to win the Jews. Verse 20 also tells us that it was to win those under the law. Verse 21 tells us that it was to win those not having the law. Verse 22 tells us it was to win the weak. Verse 22 tells us it was to save some.

Paul's great heart desire was that people would hear of his beloved Jesus who had saved and changed his life. And that, upon hearing, they would open their hearts to Him, be saved, and begin a new and transformed life of freedom in loving and serving Him.

Paul particularly wanted to reach those who had never heard. *"It has always been my ambition to preach the gospel where Christ was not known, so that I would not be building on someone else's foundation." (Romans 15:20)*

Then, using the same athletic metaphor that he later used in II Timothy, Paul says,

*"Do you not know that in a race, all the runners run, but only one gets the prize? Run in such a way as to get the prize. Everyone who competes in the games goes into strict training. They do it to get a crown that will not last; but we do it to get a crown that will last forever. Therefore, I do not run like a man running aimlessly; I do not fight like a man beating the air. No, I beat my body and make it my slave so that, after I have preached to others, I myself will not be disqualified for the prize. (I Corinthians 9:24-27)*

Paul wanted the prize. He sought the crown that will last forever. And he worked as hard as any athlete to win souls and win rewards.

Again, I don't for a moment believe that he did so for his own self-aggrandizement. He never recovered from the grace of God that exploded into his life and I imagine that his "crown that lasts forever" is already sitting at the feet of the Savior that he worked so hard to know and make known.

It is clear that whatever time, talents, treasures, or tongue that he invested in reaching the unreached, were clearly given to him by his Master. He was simply being a faithful steward of that with which he had been entrusted. And, like the faithful stewards of Matthew 25 who invested their master's resources wisely, I believe Paul has heard his master's pronouncement: *"Well done, good and faithful servant! You have been faithful with a few things; you will be put in charge of many things. Come and share your master's happiness!" (Matthew 25:21)*

My prayer is that you and I, ordinary people, having invested that which the Master entrusted to us to achieve that which the Master expected from us, will hear that same commendation: *"Well done, good and faithful servant! ...Come and share your master's happiness!"*

# Chapter - 11
# CONCLUSION:
# FOR SUCH A TIME AS THIS

Hadassah was young, beautiful, Jewish, an orphan adopted by her older cousin, and totally unaware of the life-changing and eternity-changing plan that God had for her in the history of the nation of Israel and the salvation of the world. That history introduces us to Hadassah, who we are told went by the nickname Esther, after Israel's Babylonian captivity.

After being established under Saul, David, and Solomon, the kingdom of Israel split in the 10th century BC after Solomon's son, Rehoboam, followed bad advice given by unwise advisers and lost the opportunity to reign over a united 12-tribe kingdom.

The northern ten tribes called Israel followed a succession of kings who were each more evil than the one before until God gave them over to be conquered by the Assyrians in 721 BC. The Assyrians took a percentage of the population captive, brought them to Assyria to mix into the population, and forced some Assyrians to relocate to the area around Samaria. They forced mixed marriages and mixed religions with the remaining inhabitants. These were the ancestors of the Samaritans mentioned in John 4. They were seen by Jewish purists as "half-breeds" and "heretics".

The southern two tribes called Judah spent a few centuries riding a roller coaster of good-then-bad kings and godly-then-apostate leaders until God gave them over to be conquered and brought into exile by the Babylonians in 586 BC.

The Book of Esther records events during that exilic period during which the land of Israel contained only a loose remnant bearing no resemblance to the powerful, rich, and heady days of Kings David and Solomon.

The Assyrians were good at conquering people, but bad at ruling them. This led to the need for the Assyrians to return to battle in lands they had previously subjugated when local sentiments and nationalism rose up along with the people.

The Babylonians learned from Assyrian troubles. The Babylonian strategy was to go through great efforts to turn their subjected people into cultural Babylonians. They took the brightest and best of the conquered peoples and assimilated them into Babylonian culture and education (see the Book of Daniel). Remaining a faithful Jew during this intensive inculcation took remarkable resolve and a wise willingness to embrace that which one could without sinning but draw a line beyond which one would not step even at the risk of wealth, comfort, or life.

As the Babylonians were losing their exalted position of world supremacy, the Persians rose to become the dominant power. It was into this Persian empire that Esther was born in Susa in the sixth century BC.

The Persians permitted the return of some Jews to Israel which began under Zerubbabel as governor and Joshua as priest. Those two led a group to Jerusalem and rebuilt the temple to their God, YAHWEH (Jehovah).

Between that first returning remanent and the more famous one under Nehemiah as governor and Ezra as priest, the events covered in the book of Esther took place. That second return would never have been possible were it not for the salvation of the Jews made possible by Esther's seizing of the opportunity provided to her by God's providential superintendence.

Esther's opportunity to serve only became available because God had orchestrated her rise to prominence in the palace of Xerxes, also called Ahasuerus. King Xerxes was as prideful as he was powerful. He *"ruled over 127 provinces stretching from India to Kush (Ethiopia)" (Esther 1:1)*. Three years into his reign he set out to show off his vast wealth and power by throwing a five-month party with opulent displays of decadence capped by a seven-day banquet with an unlimited open bar.

In a likely-drunken moment of swagger and trying to further impress his likely-drunken friends, Xerxes beckoned his queen Vashti from her palace apartment where she was entertaining royal women from throughout the Persian empire. His goal? To parade her like he proudly showed off all his other beautiful possessions.

Vashti was having none of it!

At her refusal of this piggish request, Xerxes burned with the anger of a man with a wounded pride who was spurned in front of all the men he wanted to impress. Like a petulant child who did not get his way, he declared an edict that if Vashti didn't want to come to him then, she would never come into his presence again.

That rash vow may have temporarily satisfied his anger, but it didn't satisfy his need for a new queen. Enter Esther. Through a series of displays of God's superintendence and against humanly insurmountable odds, Esther became queen. She had won the favor of Mordecai (2:7), the favor of those who pre-selected girls to go to the palace (2:8), the favor of Hegai who had charge of the king's harem (2:10), the favor of "everyone who saw her" (2:15) and ultimately the favor of the king (2:17). This secret Jewess was selected to be the new Persian queen just before the unveiling of an existential threat to the whole of her ancestral people, the Jews.

A court official named Haman, who might have learned his pride and ruthlessness from Xerxes' example, conspired to kill Esther's cousin and adoptive father, Mordecai. To effectuate the slaughter of this one man, Haman convinced Xerxes to condone the slaughter of all that man's people: the Jews (3:13). Unknown to Xerxes, when his signet ring sealed the new edict, it also sealed the fate of his new queen.

When the murderous anti-Semitic law was announced it drew reactions from all. Haman was euphoric. The Persian people in Susa were bewildered (3:15). Mordecai was heartbroken and crushed. *"He tore his clothes, put on sackcloth and ashes, and went into the city, wailing loudly and bitterly." (4:1)*

It was from just outside the King's gate (because he could not enter the palace while mourning) that Esther and Mordecai commenced a series of Iron Age text messages that comprise the most famous verses in Esther's story. Mordecai challenges Esther to *"go into the King's presence to beg for mercy and plead with him for her people"* (4:8).

Could Mordecai have foreseen the far-reaching impact of Haman's plot and the futility of any other strategy to confound it other than Esther approaching the king? If Esther did not approach the king, then the plot would succeed. If the plot succeeded, then the Jewish people would be annihilated. If the Jewish people were annihilated, then the messianic line would cease. If the messianic line were to cease the promised Messiah who would come to save the world from sin would not come. The downstream consequence of allowing this scheme to succeed seemed to be the thwarting of God's plan for salvation to come to the Jew and the Gentile alike.

God's plan would not be thwarted!

Esther responded to Mordecai's challenge with the hesitance that could be expected and understood. An un-summoned approach to Xerxes, if met with a lack of favor, would mean her death... And the death of all Jews.

At this moment, it was addressing her exalted position as queen, her unique opportunity to make a difference in the world, and her hesitant paralysis of fear that Mordecai writes the words that echo through the last 2500 years and reach our ears to challenge us, too: *"And who knows but that you have come to royal position for such a time as this?"* (4:14).

In other words, he is saying, "Esther, God is going to do his work and it sure seems like he is going to use you. Look back. He has providentially moved in your life in the distant past when you were but a child and God brought you to me to be saved. He providentially moved in your rise to be the queen giving you favor like Joseph each step of the way and with each person you needed to usher you to this place. But it makes no difference that you are in an opportune position if you don't respond to the opportunity it affords. God did his part in getting you here. Now, will you do your part?"

"This beautiful Jewish girl of long ago, though she herself may not have known it, yet played her part in paving the way for the coming of the world's savior." (Henry H Halley)

Esther said yes!

Her yes was not without the knowledge of the possible consequences: "*I will go to the king, even though it is against the law. And if I perish, I perish*" (4:16). Her yes was not without fear. And her yes was not without the Lord.

Esther resolved to bring the petition to the King of Persia, but not before she and her friends brought a petition to the King of Kings. *"Then Esther sent this reply to Mordecai: 'Go, gather together all the Jews who are in Susa, and fast for me. Do not eat or drink for three days, night or day. I and my maids will fast as you do. When this is done, I will go to the king…"* (4:15-16). She first seeks God's favor by fasting and prayer and then, and only then, does she have hope to obtain the favor of the king.

And, by the favor and grace of God, she received the favor and grace of the king. Her faith-filled, act set in motion God's plan to thwart Haman's evil plot, save the Jews from annihilation, and continue the messianic line that led to Jesus.

Jesus came, he did the work to provide salvation and he commissioned us to make disciples of all nations because *"it is not God's will that any should perish but that all should come to repentance." (II Peter 3:9)*

We have been under God's intense favor and blessing. And so, prayerfully as Esther, faithfully as Esther, committedly as Esther we are faced with the immense needs of unreached people who, like the Jews of Esther's time, are under a curse and set to be annihilated.

Look back on God's superintending your life to get you to this very moment. As we each look at the blessed position into which God has providentially placed us, let's seek His direction for how many unreached people we can reach.

Esther had many reasons to do what she did.

If you have read this far, you have many reasons to become actively involved in helping ensure that unreached people are reached with God's love and Good News. What will you do?

*"And who knows but that you have come to royal position for such a time as this?"*

## Part Two

# RESPONSES

# Chapter - 12
# RESPONSES

We've heard the REASONS. What should be the RESPONSES?

I've laid out 10 reasons why, I believe, each of us who have heard, understood, and accepted the salvation that God offers by grace through faith in Jesus should do something to help get God's offer to those who have never heard and those who have never responded.

So, how should we respond to the first part of this book?

I do not pretend to know the precise path on which God will lead you in response to these truths. But I know how He has led me.

In Part Two of this book, which follows this page, I will share with you briefly how the Lord has led me, my wife, and many other believers to respond and launch a ministry to reach unreached people around the world. And I will invite you to join us as we work to bring God's love and Good News to the world's least-reached people.

If, at any time, you are led to join us, please return the enclosed Response Card, go to www.worldlinkonline.org, or call Worldlink at 1-610-630-3775. To have interested friends receive a free copy of *Reasons* have them go to that same site or call that same number.

# Chapter - 13
# A Tale of Two Strategies

In Part One of *REASONS*, we examined 10 reasons why we should be involved in bringing the Good News of Jesus to the unreached and the unconvinced.

So, what's the best way to reach the unreached masses of lost and hurting people around the world whom God has commissioned us to reach?

For years, I thought the only way was to go as a Western missionary. Over 40 years ago, my wife, Nancy, and I decided to do just that. But God never opened that door. Then, over the years, I met indigenous Christians all over the world who were fulfilling the mission in their own countries and doing the same work I would have done as a Western missionary.

I compared these indigenous missionaries to me and considered two strategies for reaching the unreached with the Good News.

- They already knew their language perfectly, but I would need years to learn it and a lifetime to master it.

- They were cultural insiders, while I would always be an outsider in my thinking and in the view of the local people.

- They were ready to serve immediately, whereas it would take me years to decide where to go, learn the language, raise funds, move my family, and be set to do the work.

- They would stay on mission for a lifetime, while my ministry in their country would probably end in 10 or 20 years.

- They had ministry continuity in their home country, while I would have planned to return to my home country every few years for visits, fundraising, education, and rest.

- They lived simply on the level of their peers, while even if I drastically lowered my American standard of living, it would still likely be drastically higher than those I would serve.

- They could live on a few US dollars per day, while the cost to send me and my family as Western missionaries would average hundreds of dollars a day.

I knew that God would continue to call some Westerners to relocate and serve God in other lands, but as I continued to get to know these highly qualified, deeply passionate, and clearly called indigenous missionaries, God began to clarify a new mission strategy in my heart.

So, understanding all the "REASONS" that we should be actively involved in assuring God's love and Good News is shared with the world, and seeing the unique qualifications and advantages of indigenous missionaries in their own countries, I began to see something over and over.

In my visits to countries around the world, I saw amazing ministry opportunities for my indigenous missionary brothers and sisters, but I saw them struggling for resources (a $30, $50, or $100/month salary, a bike or motorcycle, a few books to study or pamphlets to hand out...). Then I would return to the US or visit the UK and I saw vast resources in the hands of my Christian brothers and sisters, but they had no opportunity or calling to relocate to the least-reached areas of the world.

Simply put, I saw **opportunities without resources** and **resources without opportunities**. And I did a dangerous thing. I told God, "You've got to do something about that!" **He did.**

He led us to start Worldlink. Our mission is to link indigenous missionaries with the resources they need to fulfill God's Great Commission and bring his love and Good News to lost and hurting people in their own lands.

In the past 20 years, God has grown our Indigenous Missionary teams. At the time that I am writing this book, we have over 1,300 Indigenous Missionary Partners in 49 countries. It is amazing to see what God can do when we pair opportunities and resources to empower front-line indigenous missionaries in Asia, Africa, and Latin America. Every day, God is bearing fruit through the humble and faithful ministries of our indigenous brothers and sisters who are missionaries in their own countries.

# Chapter - 14
# What We Are Working Toward

Indigenous missionaries can effectively and efficiently reach unreached people and fulfill the Great Commission. We plan to grow our team of indigenous missionary partners as far as the Lord will take us. To do so, we have now clarified three **Strategic Priorities**.

# Priority 1:

## MISSIONARIES

### (To Identify, Recruit, and Support Indigenous Missionaries in Ever-Growing Numbers)

The mission-critical element in bringing the love of God and the Good News of Jesus to unreached people is a person who can model new life and explain God and his offer to those who need to hear. We know we are not called to be all things to all people, despite our hearts' desires to serve every opportunity that we encounter. To best follow what the Lord has specifically commissioned Worldlink to do, we will bring on more indigenous missionary partners to our team who are an excellent fit for our mission and values.

Over the last 20 years, Worldlink has developed a relational network of missionary contacts that assists us in locating high-quality missionary partners that meet our criteria. We have

Regional Coordinators in the Africa, Asia, and Americas regions that oversee the growing work in those areas. We have team leaders that report to our Regional Coordinators and maintain personal relationships with each of the missionaries. The Regional Coordinators and team leaders both provide recommendations for new partners and assist us with oversight of current missionary partners.

The following criteria are the essentials to which any group or individual must adhere in order to be considered for partnership. All elements must be agreed to at the launch of and upheld in the course of our ministry together. These elements have been with Worldlink since our inception and are unlikely to change.

- **Christian:** The partnering staff must be followers of Christ and agree with Worldlink's Statement of Beliefs and doctrinal positions. The elements of this statement are consistent with our understanding of Scripture and the Christian Church's historical doctrines.

- **Evangelistic:** Worldlink's international partners must have the salvation of souls as a primary emphasis in their efforts. We applaud and encourage efforts to share God's love in tangible ways, and we employ many efforts to promote pain relief and social/societal change in order to support our partners in their ongoing ministry. But our unique calling is to expand the Kingdom of God by supporting intentional evangelistic and disciple-making efforts.

- **Indigenously led:** We believe Christians born and raised in their local context are better equipped to share the Gospel in faithful, effective, and God-honoring ways that are easily understood by their culture. We want to encourage and empower their efforts, not direct, or control them from afar.

- **Leveraged:** Worldlink supports God's workers doing God's work. However, while Worldlink provides much of the financial support for most supported missionaries, we encourage and equip partners to animate local generosity as a part of growing spiritual maturity. Because local support allows greater ownership and commitment to ministry efforts by the community, this involves the community in what God is doing and models Biblical stewardship.

- **Areas less influenced by The Gospel:** This makes sense for both Worldlink's calling and our partner's lived experiences. We are interested in evangelism and discipleship and desire to fulfill Christ's last command to carry His Good News into all the world. Partners serving in areas with little or no Christian presence are in greater need of the financial, material, and spiritual partnership that Worldlink can offer.

- **A Clear and Demonstrated Calling:** Worldlink is looking for brothers and sisters who believe, with confirmation from respected people who know them best, that God is asking them to do the ministry and who are already actively serving while looking to the Lord for provision. Most often they are actively volunteering or serving with minimal support or in a bi-vocational ministry. We are not interested in workers looking for a "job;" we are interested in partnering with those following a "calling." He or she will have a reputation for being a servant and exhibit a heart of perseverance through whatever hardships might accompany the work.

111

- **Recommendation:** Worldlink will consider the possibility of a partnership with individuals and/or groups for whom we receive recommendations from our network of trusted ministry contacts around the world. We do not consider self-recommendations.

- **Commendable Character:** Those who work with potential partners should be able to say without hesitation, "This person is of such high Christian character that I have complete confidence they will do what they say and will honestly report what they did and did not accomplish."

# Priority 2:

## TRAINING

**(To Train Indigenous Missionaries for Ever-Growing Effectiveness)**

To ensure that all our partners have the ministry-appropriate biblical, theological, and practical training required to serve to their highest and best ability, we have identified 10 Core Modules that we make available by various methods to all indigenous missionary partners. These include:

- Bible Study Methods and Interpretation
- Old Testament Survey
- New Testament Survey
- Bible Doctrine
- Preaching, Teaching, and Ministry
- Personal Spiritual Life of a Missionary

- Mission and Outreach
- Church History (both Global and Local)
- Comparative Religions and Apologetics
- Pioneer Church Planting

Training and equipping of missionaries is based on the very individual needs of the missionary and the context in which they serve. Since we always work with local teams, we find that the recommended workers often come with the capacity to do significant ministry in their own context. In most cases though, additional learning can be helpful for ministry effectiveness, so the local teams can recommend necessary training. Everyone will have different needs based on the scope of their ministry, but all are required to have basic Bible training.

The level of training is higher for some than for others. For example, a simple village preacher/church planter in India requires much less training to get started than a worker evangelizing college students in an African city.

Additionally, we share best practices between regions. For example, what is successful in evangelism in Indonesia might also be applicable to the northern tier of sub-Saharan Africa. We are able to cross-pollinate ideas from around the world.

## Missionary training is available through three opportunities:

**Missionary Training Centers (MTC)** are 11-month residential training centers that train pioneer evangelists and church planters and then send them out to unreached people groups living in remote and hard places. A Missionary Training Center is not for those who seek degrees but rather for those who are called by God into pioneer evangelism and church planting. Partners that are a good fit for this modality can immerse themselves in intensive missionary training which provides sound theology as well as tools and practical evangelism and church-planting methods. After completion, the graduates are sent to unreached people groups to evangelize and plant churches.

**Missionary Training Institutes (MTI)** provide similar training in a non-residential format for those whose ministry or family responsibilities preclude the MTC experience. MTIs are held in short sessions (5-7 days) over a longer period (one session every three months) in dispersed areas (mostly local churches) so that missionaries can have access to training while still continuing their ministry.

**Missionary Training Materials (MTM)** are provided for those who already have training or for those who cannot study in English or one of the languages in which training is offered. Our partners are regularly involved in writing or translating materials into languages best understood by indigenous missionaries.

# Priority 3:

## SPECIAL PROJECTS

### (To Deepen the Impact of Indigenous Missionaries Through Special Projects)

In order to maximize our efforts and resources for reaching the unreached, we periodically pursue high-return-on-investment special projects. In the past, these have included buying Bibles and Christian literature for distribution, purchasing vehicles (bikes, motorbikes, cars, vans), building church buildings, ministry centers, and children's homes, constructing missionary training centers, educating orphaned/abandoned/abused children, digging wells, providing support for widows of martyred partners, offering emergency relief and support, and publishing and distributing books, audiobooks, and documentary films.

Additionally, for those called to reach their countrymen and women, other needs are wide and varied. Worldlink seeks to provide whatever is needed to overcome barriers to their effective witness. This support may go well beyond salary support or supplement and include training and sharing of best practices, strategic planning assistance, equipment, pastoral encouragement and support, and spiritual support through prayer and intercession. It's often a lonely road for these faithful servants who are living in areas with little or no Christian presence. It is wonderful for our partners to know that a team of like-minded brothers and sisters from around the world is supporting them in prayer and is available to encourage them.

To provide this exponentially expanding support we continue to add high-performance members to our Home Team and grow our technological and relational footprint in the USA and UK.

# Chapter - 15
# Why We Support Indigenous Missionaries

My friend and colleague in ministry, Dr. CV John, and I both have our spiritual roots in a group of churches that tend to get great pleasure out of preaching outlines that are alliterated. So, unable to help ourselves, we came up with the following 10 reasons why we support the strategy of reaching the unreached through empowering partnerships with indigenous missionaries. Enjoy, all you alliteration lovers.

## Indigenous missionaries are:

- **Sensitive Culturally**

  Indigenous missionaries understand the culture and the thinking of the nearby people they are reaching and can apply the truth of God using (or avoiding) words, phrases, and illustrations in ways that would be unknown to an outsider.

- **Superior Linguistically**

  While it would take two to five years for a foreigner to learn a new language and a lifetime to achieve fluency, indigenous missionaries can speak their local languages fluently and immediately.

- **Suited Educationally**

  Front-line outreach work in most of the world does not require the high educational standards of most Western missionary organizations. In fact, sometimes the simple truth of the Good News gets lost within educated speech and arguments. Local indigenous ministers are often ideally suited to serve local unreached people due to having the same level of education and experience as the people they are serving and to whom they minister.

- **Stout Physically**

  Local Christians are quite used to the difficult living and ministry conditions in which they serve because they grew up in those conditions.

- **Sympathetic Socially**

  A local, indigenous missionary will live at the social/financial level of the people to whom they are bringing the Good News, creating a commonality, and resulting in openness.

- **Secure Politically**

  While Indigenous missionaries serving in their home country are subject to greater persecution than Westerners, they will not be deported or denied entry because they are residents of their country of citizenship.

- **Simple Organizationally**

  The organization of indigenous missionaries fits the unelaborate cultural and relational norms of the local area without layers of complexity imposed from outside their context.

- **Steadfast Passionately**

  The local missionary has a passion to reach their own tribes and own country because they are his or her own "family."

117

- **Strong Spiritually**

  Indigenous missionaries have some of the strongest faith in the world.

- **Sound Economically**

  Indigenous missionaries are remarkably cost-efficient because of their low salary needs, their ability to live in local- standard housing and eat local foods, their minimal transportation needs while traveling on foot or by bike or public transport, and the lack of required international travel/insurance/ visas or international education for their children.

# Chapter - 16
# Worldlink's Statement of Beliefs

We ask it all the time: "Why reinvent the wheel?" I try not to unless the wheel doesn't work.

When we started Worldlink, we needed a Statement of Beliefs that expressed our understanding of Scripture simply enough, yet completely enough, that everyone from the theologians on the board to the village church planters could understand and agree with it. It was quite easy to find because I had been working for a decade with a ministry that had exactly that kind of statement.

So, with permission, we did not reinvent the Statement of Beliefs. We installed an identical one and started driving.

Worldlink International Ministries accepts and proclaims the historic truths of the Christian faith including the following:

## God and the Human Race

**We** hold that the Lord our God is one: Father, Son, and Holy Spirit, and that he fulfills his sovereign purposes in creation, revelation, redemption, judgment, and the coming of his kingdom by calling out from the world a people united to himself and to each other in love.

**We** acknowledge that though God made us in his own likeness and image, conferring on us dignity and worth and enabling us to respond to Himself, we now are members of a fallen race; we have sinned and come short of his glory.

**We** believe that the Father has shown us his holy love in giving Jesus Christ, his only Son, for us, while through our sinfulness and guilt, we were subject to his wrath and condemnation, and has shown his grace by putting sinners right with himself when they place their trust in his Son.

**We** confess Jesus Christ as Lord and God; as truly human, born of the virgin Mary; as Servant, sinless, full of grace and truth; as only Mediator and Savior, dying on the cross in our place, representing us to God, redeeming us from the grip, guilt, and punishment of sin; as Victor over Satan and all his forces, rising from death with a glorious body, being taken up to be with his Father, one day returning personally in glory and judgment to establish his kingdom.

**We** believe in the Holy Spirit who convicts the world in regard to sin, righteousness, and judgment; who makes the death of Christ effective to sinners, declaring that they must now turn to Christ in repentance and directing their trust towards the Lord Jesus Christ; who through the new birth makes us partake in the life of the risen Christ, and who is present within all believers, illuminating their minds to grasp the truth of Scripture, producing in them his fruit, granting to them his gifts, and empowering them for service in the world.

## The Scriptures

**We** believe that the Old and New Testament Scriptures are God-breathed, since their writers spoke from God as they were moved by the Holy Spirit; hence are fully trustworthy in all that they affirm; and are our highest authority for faith and life.

# The Church and Its Mission

**We** recognize the Church as the body of Christ, held together and growing up in him; both as a total fellowship throughout the world, and as the local congregation in which believers gather.

**We** acknowledge the commission of Christ to proclaim the Good News to all people, making them disciples, and teaching them to obey him.

**We** acknowledge the command of Christ to love our neighbors, resulting in service to the church and society, in seeking reconciliation for all with God and their fellows, in proclaiming liberty from every kind of oppression; and in spreading Christ's justice in an unjust world … until he comes again.

# Chapter - 17
# Worldlink's Working Principles

Every year, each member of the Worldlink Board of Directors reviews and affirms their agreement with, and commitment to, Worldlink's Statement of Beliefs and Statement of Working Principles. It is upon these truths and our shared understanding that we join in shared ministry at Worldlink.

We affirm these basic principles upon which we have built and continue to build Worldlink.

## These are our Worldlink Working Principles:

1. God wants this generation of believers to bring his tangible love and Good News to this generation of unbelievers worldwide.

2. God has made available to his church all the resources required to accomplish this task.

3. Indigenous missionaries are uniquely positioned to effectively bring God's love and the Gospel to the people of their own countries.

4. Partnerships that equip and empower indigenous missionaries are an effective strategy for spreading the Good News.

5. Christians around the world have been given stewardship of a vast amount of God's resources that he wants to use to reach the world for Christ.

6. Christians around the world can be motivated to invest God's resources in support of their brothers and sisters on the frontlines of indigenous missionary service.

7. Worldlink can efficiently link God's people and resources with God's servants in the majority world.

8. Worldlink will send 100% of funds designated for indigenous missionaries to directly support our partners in the field.

9. God wants Worldlink to continue to grow the number of people reached by continuing to grow the number of indigenous missionaries supported.

10. To grow the number of indigenous missionaries supported we must continually increase the impact of prayer and financial partners.

11. A godly, passionate, capable, and equipped Board and Staff are critical to the success of Worldlink's endeavors.

12. Only with the direction of God and the empowerment of his Spirit will our efforts be fruitful.

# Chapter - 18
# Frequently Asked Questions

## What is an indigenous missionary?

From a Christian perspective, a missionary is a Christian on a mission to share the love of God and the Good News of Jesus Christ with other people. Some people associate the term "missionary" with a person sharing God's love in another culture or another country. This is not required in the Bible or in today's world.

Worldlink uses the terms indigenous missionary, native missionary, and local missionary to help define our international partners. They are missionaries to the people in the land in which they were born and live.

## Where are Worldlink's indigenous missionary partners located?

Simply put, our partners serve in areas with the "Greatest Need and Least Access." Philosophically, our partnerships focus on areas where the local population is unreached or less reached with the Good News. Geographically, this currently includes the following countries:

- **Asia Region:** Bangladesh, Bhutan, Cambodia, India, Indonesia, Laos, Myanmar, Nepal, Pakistan, and Sri Lanka, and restrictive countries that I will not name.

124

- **Americas Region:** Colombia, Dominican Republic, Guatemala, El Salvador, Haiti, and restrictive countries that I will not name.

- **Africa Region:** Benin, Burkina Faso, Cameroon, Central African Republic, Chad, Congo, Democratic Republic of the Congo, Eswatini, Ethiopia, Gambia, Ghana, Ivory Coast, Kenya, Lesotho, Liberia, Malawi, Mali, Mauritius, Mauritania, Mozambique, Nigeria, Rwanda, Senegal, Sierra Leone, South Africa, South Sudan, Tanzania, Togo, Uganda, Zambia and Zimbabwe.

## What advantages do indigenous missionaries have?

Because they are native to the places they serve, there are numerous, significant advantages that indigenous missionaries have over traditional Western missionaries.

- Indigenous missionaries are often more effective than their Western counterparts because they have no language, culture, travel, or lifestyle barriers to overcome.

- Indigenous missionaries can live, serve, and travel in closed countries that cannot be reached by Western missionaries.

- Indigenous missionaries do not need to leave the "mission field" for long periods of rest or to raise support back home - since they are already home.

- Indigenous missionaries do not need to abandon their work when regional conflicts or worldwide pandemics arise.

- The work of indigenous missionaries is highly cost-effective. While it costs an average of $40,000 US to $70,000 US a year to support the typical Western missionary, an indigenous missionary can be fully supported for as little as $400US to $2,000 US a year.

# How do you train your missionaries?

Training and equipping of missionaries are based on the individual needs of the missionaries and the context in which they serve. Since we always work with local teams, we find that the recommended partners often come with the capacity to do significant ministry in their own context. In most cases though, additional learning can be helpful for ministry effectiveness, so the local teams can recommend necessary training. Everyone will have different needs based on the scope of their ministry, but all are required to have basic Bible training.

The level of training is higher for some than for others. For example, a village preacher/church planter in India requires much less training to get started than a worker evangelizing college students in an African city.

Additionally, we share best practices between regions. For example, what is successful in evangelism in Indonesia might also be applicable to the northern tier of sub-Saharan Africa. We are able to cross-pollinate ideas from around the world.

# What are Worldlink's indigenous missionary partners doing?

Our partners work in three areas of emphasis that each aim to bring the Good News of Jesus to receptive hearts.

- **Outreach.** Often the hearts of spiritually needy people are open to hearing of God's grace, so our partners are running evangelistic clubs in Pakistan, Jesus film outreaches in Uganda, Gospel campaigns in Ethiopia, church planting ministries in Indonesia, Bible listening groups in Tanzania, prison visitation in Zambia, Mobile Bible Institute training in India, athletic outreaches in Kenya, and so much more.

126

- **Mercy.** Often experiencing a touch of God's love is the first step in people's openness to hearing his Good News, so our partners are rescuing victims of war-ignited sexual violence in the Democratic Republic of the Congo, relieving suffering in refugee settlements in Sri Lanka, aiding the persecuted in Nigeria, feeding children in Guatemalan villages, and so much more.

- **Children.** Often the most receptive hearts are the youngest hearts, so our partners are leading Bible camps in Nigeria, life skills seminars in Togo, children's homes in India, orphan ministry in Rwanda, ministry to slum children in Colombia, outreaches to former child soldiers in Sierra Leone, school peer Bible clubs in Liberia, Vacation Bible clubs in Nepal, and so much more.

## How do you support your missionaries with supplies?

As with training, supplies are based on individual partner or ministry needs. We generally do not send equipment or materials from the West to our missionary partners. We have found that if supplies are needed, they are better if locally procured. This eliminates the problem of "Western" materials being introduced into the context, helps our indigenous missionary partners cultivate relationships with vendors from whom they buy supplies, and aids the local economy. So, when we want to provide bicycles for indigenous missionary evangelists, we do not load a container of bikes and send them over. We send the money to purchase them locally. In this way, the relief is immediate, less expensive, and contextually acceptable.

Further more, in many of the cultures in which front-line indigenous missionaries serve it is not a benefit to be associated with Western entities. If an indigenous missionary is seen as connected to Western money, ideas, and direction, it tends to produce suspicion of motives and opens the missionary to targeting by maliciously minded opponents.

## How do you distribute funds to your missionaries?

We distribute funds to our partners either monthly or quarterly depending on the local circumstances. Our policy is that 100% of funds that are raised and designated for our indigenous missionary partners or specific ministries/projects, go to that partner/ministry. We raise all funds for operational and administrative support separately.

## How does Worldlink find its indigenous partners?

Through long-standing ministry relationships with indigenous Christian leaders in the developing world, Worldlink has been able to construct reliable webs of relationships that allow us to connect with Christian workers of high character and giftedness for ministry. A thorough process of evaluation, including independent references, is undertaken prior to accepting anyone for partnership.

Many of our relationships began with Jack Nelson, our founder and president, and contacts from his decade of service with Scripture Union (an evangelistic and Bible engagement ministry, active in over 120 countries). During that time, Jack developed relationships with respected church and ministry leaders in countries around the world. When God led him to start Worldlink, he went to his trusted friends/colleagues to locate people who were ready to be full-time indigenous missionaries in their own countries.

Since those early days, we have seen our network of trusted advocates expand and now new missionary partners come to us at the recommendation of trusted Christian leaders worldwide (primarily through current Worldlink partners) who can vouch for their character, capability, chemistry, and calling.

## What are Worldlink's partnership preferences?

Our partnerships may change over time based on God's leading, strategic timing, and opportunity. We may prefer a certain geographical region for several reasons. We may sense God's leading toward a particular opportunity that may close rapidly. Based upon a variety of factors, partnerships might be one-time, decreasing over time, or ongoing.

Worldlink does not generally partner with established churches in other countries. This is because faithful giving of the local congregation allows for financial support of that local ministry, but, in the areas where we work, local funds are not generally available to missionaries who are planting churches in unreached regions or operating alongside churches.

Church planters who plan to become pastors will be considered for decreasing financial partnerships. This is based on the understanding that many groups focus evangelistic efforts on creating churches in areas where none exist. Support for these efforts would be required and appropriate. This financial support will be decreased over time as the Gospel takes hold in the community and the church is able to support the work of its minister.

## What are the major needs of indigenous missionaries?

For those called to reach their countrymen and women, the needs are wide and varied. Worldlink seeks to provide whatever is needed to overcome barriers to their effective witness. This support may include salary support or supplement; training and sharing of best practices; strategic planning assistance; equipment; pastoral encouragement and support; and prayerful and spiritual support. It's often a lonely road for these faithful servants who are living in areas with little or no Christian presence. It is wonderful for our partners to know that a team from around the world is supporting them in prayer and is available to encourage them.

Typically, support includes a small amount of money that is added to locally available support to equal a full-time salary (freeing indigenous missionaries from the daily concern of feeding and sheltering themselves and their families). It also includes helping with additional training. Our networks allow us to connect national Christian workers with opportunities for help with things such as evangelism in a particular religious or anti-religious context, local fundraising, educational opportunities when opposing forces deny them - especially helping with biblical and doctrinal education, equipment for more effective ministry, and equipment for ministry travel needs.

## Why is Worldlink a good option for supporting indigenous missionaries? To whom is Worldlink accountable?

Worldlink is committed to *"taking pains to do what is right, not only in the eyes of the Lord but also in the eyes of men."* *(2 Corinthians 8:21)*

Worldlink is led by an independent Board of Directors. Classified by the United States Internal Revenue Service (IRS) as a non-profit 501(c) 3 organization, Worldlink is accountable to both Pennsylvania State and US Federal regulations governing the proper use of donated funds. We are also a member in good standing with the Evangelical Council for Financial Accountability (www.ECFA.org), and we abide by their Seven Standards of Responsible Stewardship (www.ECFA.org/Content/7Standards. as px).

Every year an independent accounting firm audits our financial records. These audits are available for public inspection at our office.

## How much does Worldlink withhold from funds donated to the ministry of international Partners?

Nothing. (That is 0%.)

From its inception, Worldlink has been committed to sending 100% of the money received for international partners to our international partners. This has been and will continue to be our faithful practice.

Home Team staff compensation and operating expenses are raised independently of missionary support.

## How are the indigenous missionary partners held accountable?

We agree with an Indian friend who said that accountability is "not a 'Western' thing, not an 'Eastern' thing, but a Jesus thing." Consequently, we expect our partners to regularly inform us about three areas of their lives, following the example of the Apostle Paul:

*Tychicus, the dear brother and faithful servant in the Lord, will tell you everything, so that you may know **how I am** and **what I am doing**. I am sending him to you for this very purpose, that you may know how we are and that he may encourage you. (Ephesians 6:21-22)*

*...they sailed back to Antioch where they had been committed to the grace of God for the work they had now completed. On arriving there, they gathered the church together and reported **all that God had done** through them and how he had opened the door of faith to the Gentiles. (Acts 14:26-27)*

Our international accountability structure includes:

• Quarterly reports based on the topics mentioned above including, 1) How are the partners and their families doing physically, emotionally, and spiritually, 2) What activities have they done this quarter and what is planned for the next, and 3) What results has God brought through the ministry?

• Site visits by area and regional leadership staff

• Site visits by Worldlink US or UK staff

• Review by local contacts

• Significant pre-partnership analysis, prayer, and research (getting the right people and commitments at the start means better relationships down the road).

## How does Worldlink address the concern of dependency?

First, we acknowledge that we are all dependent on something or someone. Every right-minded Christian will acknowledge that we are dependent on God. The question is not whether or not we, our missionary partners, or anyone else, are dependent, but rather "upon whom or what are we dependent?"

Worldlink's international partners, as well as our US and UK staff, look to God rather than to people for sustenance. We are constantly watching our interactions to make sure that we support their ministry goals rather than dictate Western solutions to local concerns.

It is popular to talk about the "three selves" in the global church: self-governing, self-propagating, and self-supporting. Worldlink believes that when the first two are true and healthy, the third is not much of an issue.

Dependency can be an unnecessary distraction, or even an excuse, for some Western Christians. We have never heard someone bemoan the fact that a local Western pastor is entirely dependent on the local congregation for their income. We have never heard of someone concerned that an inner-city ministry in a poor area of town is funded through a partnership with a suburban church. We have never seen angst in someone over the fact that an outreach ministry in an impoverished rural area is supported through funding from other areas. We have never heard a missions committee express trepidation over "creating dependency" in the lives and ministries of the Western missionaries they are supporting in another part of the world. So, why is it that "creating dependency" is only an issue when we are discussing supporting people who are different from us? Perhaps the real issue is based on a lack of trust or lack of control.

All funds in the hands of God's people really belong to God. We are not sure that God is awfully concerned whether support for his work comes from a pocket that is 10 feet from the offering plate, 10 miles from the offering plate, or 10 time zones from the offering plate. As long as the minister receiving the funds in support of his or her ministry realizes that all support funds are from the hand of God and it is God, and God alone, upon which the minister is dependent, then which pocket God pulls those funds from is of little consequence.

## How can I help Worldlink and its indigenous missionary partners?

First, pray without ceasing. Use the monthly Prayerlink as your guide. The Prayerlink is designed to guide you through daily prayer and intercession for our partners and our ministry; each month there are new requests from around the world. It is also a great way to stay up to date on ongoing ministries and the status of our partners.

You can receive your copy monthly by signing up on the Worldlink website at worldlinkonline.org.

Second, be extravagantly generous in your donations. The opportunities that Worldlink's current and prospective indigenous missionary partners have to reach people for Christ far outpace the funds that we currently have to empower them. If you are led, any gifts would be incredibly helpful. Go to the Worldlink website at www.worldlinkonline.org or send in the response card found in this book to support an indigenous missionary. Remember that 100% of funds sent for indigenous missionaries go to that missionary.

Third, become a Worldlink advocate. If you agree with what you've read in this book, tell others of the amazing things God is doing and the amazing ways they can join you and make an immediate and eternal difference in the lives of people in some of the world's hardest-to-reach places. Free copies of *Reasons* (and the companion book *Reachable*) are available on our website.

To schedule Jack Nelson, or someone else from Worldlink, to preach or share with your church or group, contact info@worldlinkonline.org.

## What have others said about Worldlink?

*"Worldlink is a ministry with a mission close to God's heart and a strategy that brings positive results with low expenses and exemplary Christian leadership. I commend Worldlink to you."*

- Dr. Philip G. Ryken, President, Wheaton College, Wheaton, IL

*"In my role as Scripture Union International Director, I oversee our work in over 120 countries. In my travels, I have seen first-hand the fruit of Worldlink's native missionary partnerships and the tremendous value and outcomes of their support. I am happy to recommend Worldlink and Jack to you without hesitation."*

-Janet Morgan, Retired International Director, Scripture Union International, London, UK

*"As a Christian, I am called to reach people around the world with the Gospel. As a business owner, I am also called to be a faithful steward of the resources God has blessed me with and to seek to get the highest return on investment of Kingdom resources. Both of these calls are satisfied in the work of Worldlink International Ministries."*

-Jeffrey Rose, President, Life Song for Orphans Haiti Advocate Board, Delray Beach, FL

*"In 2002, when the Lord led Jack to found Worldlink to help spread the Gospel in partnership with native missionaries, I was thrilled because I had experienced first-hand the effectiveness of the native missionaries with whom Jack had connected me.... Without hesitation, I encourage you to join in God's work through Worldlink with your prayers, your investment of time, and your generous financial partnership."*

-Rev. Carroll L.G. Wynne, Minister of Pastoral Care, Tenth Presbyterian Church, Philadelphia, PA

*"Put simply, if Worldlink did not exist, the forward thrust of the Gospel message would be thwarted in many strategic areas. Worldlink has my highest respect and greatest appreciation. Their work is not easy, but it is vital."*

-David Jones, Managing Director, Cedar stone, Wheaton, IL

*"Worldlink's internal controls and procedures are about as good as any I've seen... Your system is set up very well and covers all the bases and then some."*

-Georgia L.S. Myers, CPA, Director, Canon Capital Certified Public Accountants, Souderton, PA

# DISCUSSION GUIDE OFFER

Transformational Christian growth often happens best among a group of people who are interacting with a passage of Scripture, a Biblical concept, or a moving of the Holy Spirit together. A group brings unique knowledge, perspectives, experiences, and insights to bear as we wrestle to understand what we are learning and apply what we have learned.

For that reason, we have created a discussion guide for you to use in small groups, families, or churches.

To access the free REASONS DISCUSSION GUIDE, visit the Resources page of Worldlink's website (worldlinkonline.org) or use this QR Code.

## FREE BOOK OFFER

While on the website, you can also request a free copy of Jack Nelson's book, *REACHABLE: How Indigenous Missionaries Are Changing the Face of Missions*.

Some people's response to the world's unreached billions is to think that they are unreachable. Nothing could be further from the truth! When you know that they are reachable, the next question is, "How?" *REACHABLE* answers that question with inspiring stories of the lives and ministries of indigenous missionaries and a heartfelt call to be their partner.

# Appendix - 1
# The Good News of Jesus

Throughout this book, I have referred to God's Good News. I thought it would be important to share what that is to be sure we are all on the same page and can respond accordingly.

First, it's good to understand that I have used the word gospel, and the phrase "Good News" interchangeably. The reason for this is that they are exactly the same.

The Greek word translated as Gospel is "*euangelion*". It starts with the prefix "eu" which means good. Think of a eulogy at a funeral, which is saying good (eu) words (logos) about the dead person. Or eugenics, the desire for a race of people with "good" (eu) genes. Or a euphemism, which literally means good speaking, and is defined as using a better or more palatable word to describe something distasteful. Speaking of a euphemism, how about euthanasia, which combines the Greek "eu" (good) and "thanatos" (death) and purports to offer good death?

In the word "euangelion", to the prefix "eu" is added "angelion" which means a message (or messenger when it speaks of an angel). So, the gospel means a good message or good news (I capitalize it when referring to the particular title of the Good News offered in the Bible). Euangelion is also the word that becomes transliterated into our English evangelism (sharing the Good News) and evangelical (one who believes in and shares the Good News).

So, what is this Good News or Gospel?

Whenever I want to define something in the Bible, I like to go where the Bible defines it. In this case, let's go to I Corinthians 15.

*"Now, Brothers, I want to remind you of the gospel I preach to you, which you received, and on which you have taken your stand. By this gospel, you are saved... for what I received I passed on to you as of first importance: that Christ died for our sins, according to the scriptures, that he was buried, that he was raised on the third day, according to the Scriptures, and that he appeared..." (I Corinthians 15:1-4)*

The apostle Paul, the author of this text, says that the Good News is the most important thing. Paul preached the Good News. The Corinthians received the Good News. The Corinthians took their stand on the Good News. And because they heard, understood, and received it, the Corinthians were saved by the Good News.

So, what is the good message that saved them when they believed/received it?

It is that Jesus Christ died for our sins (which was proven by the fact that he was buried) and that he was raised from the dead (which was proven by the fact that he appeared after his death to many people).

Let's start where the Good News starts: *"Christ died for our sins."*

Inherent in this statement is some bad news. If Christ died for our sins, it means that we (I and you and everyone else) have sinned. So, let's ask the question. What does the Bible mean when it talks about sin?

Again, let's go to where the Bible defines the word. In I John 3:4, we read, *"Everyone who sins breaks the law; in fact, sin is lawlessness."* The Greek word translated as lawlessness is "anomia." The prefix "a" in any word negates what comes after it. For example, an atheist says there is no ("a") God ("Theos"), or an agnostic says that they have no ("a") knowledge ("gnosis") about God.

The second part of anomia is "nomia" which means law or rule or reign or will.

So, sin is the absence of the rule or reign or will of God in my life, and hence, the substitution of my will. In essence, it is saying to God, "I'm going to do what I want, when I want, where I want, and with whom I want no matter what you say."

And we all have done that at one point in our life… or thousands of points. The Bible is clear about that. In fact, earlier in that same letter, John writes, *"If we claim to be without sin, we deceive ourselves, and the truth is not in us"* and, *"if we claim we have not sinned, we make him [God] out to be a liar, and his word is not in us." (I John 1:8, 10)*

The apostle Paul expresses the bad news this way, *"for all have sinned and fallen short of the glory of God." (Romans 3:23)*

That's bad news, but there is worse news: *"The wages of sin is death." (Romans 6:23)*

When we work, the fair thing, the right thing is that we get paid, that we get the wages we've earned. When we sin, the fair thing, the right thing is that we get paid, that we get the wages we've earned.

The right/fair wages/consequences that I get when I say to God that I'm going to do things my way is death. It's important

141

that we understand that death is not the cessation of existence, but the separation in existence. When I die physically, my immaterial part is separated from my physical body. Spiritual death is when my immaterial part (soul/spirit) is separated from God. And eternal death makes that separation permanent if it is not rectified before my physical death.

Let me give you a little bit of doubly worse news: we can't rectify our separation from God on our own. We can't earn our way into forgiveness for our sins which resulted in separation from God in the first place. The apostle Paul put it this way, *"Now we know that whatever the law says, it says to those who are under the law, so that every mouth may be silenced, and the whole world held accountable to God. Therefore, no one will be declared righteous in his sight, by observing the law; rather through the law, we become conscious of sin." (Romans 3:19-20)*

God knows that we can't live up to the standards of perfection. I know it, too. It is confirmed when I look at the requirements of God's law and the requirements of my conscience. Those verify for me that I fall short of God's righteousness.

So, we've seen bad news, worse news, and even worse, worse news. Where is the Good News, the gospel we were promised? How can I be seen as righteous and reconciled to God? Here's the Good News:

*"But now, a righteousness from God, apart from the law, has been made known, to which the Law and the Prophets testify. This righteousness from God comes through faith in Jesus Christ to all who believe. There is no difference, for all have sinned and fall short of the glory of God, and are justified freely by his grace..." (Romans 3:21-24a)*

142

That's why our central text in I Corinthians 15 says that "Christ died for our sins" is the Good News.

The most famous verses in the Bible tell us, *"For God so loved the world that he gave his one and only Son, that whoever believes in him shall not perish but have eternal life. For God did not send his son into the world to condemn the world, but to save the world through him. Whoever believes in him is not condemned, but whoever does not believe stands condemned already because he has not believed in the name of God's one and only Son." (John 3:16-18)*

*"Yet to all who receive him, to those who believed in his name, he gave the right to become children of God." (John 1:12)*

*"For it is by grace you have been saved, through faith - and this is not from yourselves, it is the gift of God - not by works, so that no one can boast." (Ephesians 2:8-9)*

## I want to offer a summary of the Good News:

1. We have all sinned.

2. The wages we rightly receive as a result of our sin is separation from God.

3. We cannot be connected again to God on our own.

4. God provided the way back.

5. Jesus is the way because he died to pay the price for our sins.

6. Jesus offers us full forgiveness and reconciliation.

7. The way to obtain that forgiveness is by receiving it as a free gift by faith.

8. The choice now belongs to each of us.

a. We can choose to remain separated from God because of our sins.

b. We can choose to try to work and earn our way to forgiveness, even though God says it's impossible.

c. We can choose to, by faith, reach out and receive his free gift of salvation.

If you have reached this far in this book and find that you want to choose that third option, I'd implore you to do that. If you don't know how, let me suggest three words that start with "A" that I learned many years ago: Admit, Agree, and Accept.

Admit that you have gone your own way rather than God's way and that the result of that is that you are separated from God.

Agree that Jesus died to pay for your sins and rose again from the dead, offering you the gift of eternal life.

Accept God's free gift of salvation, without trying to earn it on your own.

Would you let him save you right now? This is the most important decision you will ever make. If you want to do that, simply tell God in prayer. You don't need special words, just tell him what's in your heart. But if you want a starting place why not say:

"God, I know I am a sinner in need of your grace. I believe that Jesus died to pay for my sins. I now accept your offer of salvation with gratitude. Help me live for you because I know you died for me."

It's a simple decision with life-changing and eternity-altering results.

# MY DECISION

If you made the decision to trust Jesus as your savior, let me suggest that you memorialize your decision by signing below.

Signed:

 Date:

If you made that decision, please let us know at info@worldlinkonline.org.

If you made that decision, you now have the privilege and responsibility of bringing God's Good News to others who have never heard of the offer you just accepted. I can think of 10 Reasons why you should consider getting started. May the Lord bless you as you do.